ADVANCED MODULAR M[...]

Pure Mathematics
2

for A and AS level
The University of London modular mathematics syllabus

Stephen Webb
for

NATIONAL
EXTENSION
COLLEGE

Collins Educational
An Imprint of HarperCollins*Publishers*

Published by Collins Educational
An imprint of HarperCollins*Publishers*
77-85 Fulham Palace Road
Hammersmith
London W6 8JB

© National Extension College Trust Ltd 1994
First published 1994
Reprinted 1998
ISBN 0 00 322395 7

This book was written by Stephen Webb for the National Extension College Trust Ltd.

Designed by Derek Lee
Cover design and implementation by Derek Lee
Page layout by Mary Bishop
Project editor, Hugh Hillyard-Parker

The author and publishers thank Pat Perkins, Joan Billington and Joe Petran for their comments on this book.

Printed and bound in Great Britain by Scotprint Ltd, Musselburgh

The National Extension College is an educational trust and a registered charity with a distinguished body of trustees. It is an independent, self-financing organisation.

Since it was established in 1963, NEC has pioneered the development of flexible learning for adults. NEC is actively developing innovative materials and systems for distance-learning options from basic skills and general education to degree and professional training.

For further details of NEC resources that support *Advanced Modular Mathematics*, and other NEC courses, contact NEC Customer Services:

National Extension College Trust Ltd
18 Brooklands Avenue
Cambridge CB2 2HN
Telephone 0223 316644, Fax 0223 313586

CONTENTS

P2

Advanced Modular Mathematics

FOREWORD This book is one of a series covering the University of London Examination and Assessment Council's modular 'A' level Mathematics syllabus. It covers all the subject material for Pure Mathematics 2 (Module P2).

While this series of text books has been structured to match the University of London (ULEAC) syllabuses, we hope that the informal style of the text and approach to important concepts will encourage other readers, whose final examinations are from other examination Boards, to use the books for extra reading and practice.

This book is meant to be *used*: read the text, study the worked examples and work through the exercises, which will give you practice in the basic skills you need for maths at this level. There are many books for advanced mathematics, which include many more exercises: use this book to direct your studies, making use of as many other resources as you can. This book will act as a bridge between your new syllabus and the many older books that can still give even more practice in advanced mathematics.

Exercises are given at the end of each section; these range from the basic to exam-type questions. Many exercises, and worked examples, are based on *applications* of the mathematics in this book. We have given answers to all problems, so that you can check your work.

The National Extension College has more experience of flexible-learning materials than any other body (see p. ii). This series is a distillation of that experience: *Advanced Modular Mathematics* helps to put you in control of your own learning.

1

Algebra

INTRODUCTION We are going to continue covering the basic techniques of algebra in this section. Later on in the module we will see how certain aspects help with some differentiation and integration problems. We will start by looking at a particular kind of relationship called an identity.

Identities

The equation $(x-1)^2 = 4$ has only two solutions for x, given by $x-1 = \pm 2 \Rightarrow x = 3$ or $x = -1$. On the other hand, an equation like $(x-1)^2 = x^2 - 2x + 1$ is always true, no matter what values of x we put in. In this case, we call it an *identity* and to distinguish this from an equation, we write it:

$$(x-1)^2 \equiv x^2 - 2x + 1$$

with an extra line in the equal sign.

Sometimes we are given an equation with some unknown coefficients and asked to find the value of the coefficients that would make the equation true for all values of x, i.e. make it an identity. Suppose, for example, that we are given

$$(x+1)(x^2 + ax + b) \equiv x^3 + 3x^2 + 5x + 3$$

What values of a and b must we choose to make the two sides equal for any value of x? There are two approaches. Either we substitute suitable values of x, probably ending up with simultaneous equations, or we multiply out the left hand side and compare the coefficients on the two sides. Let's try each of these methods.

Values

If we take $x = 1$ and put this value into both sides of the identity, we have:

$$2(1 + a + b) = 1 + 3 + 5 + 3 \quad \Rightarrow \quad 2 + 2a + 2b = 12$$
$$\Rightarrow \quad 2a + 2b = 10$$
$$\Rightarrow \quad a + b = 5 \qquad \ldots \text{①}$$

1

Then taking $x = 2$,

$$3(4 + 2a + b) = 8 + 12 + 10 + 3 \qquad \Rightarrow \qquad 12 + 6a + 3b = 33$$
$$\Rightarrow \qquad 6a + 3b = 21$$
$$\Rightarrow \qquad 2a + b = 7 \qquad \dots \text{②}$$

Subtracting ① from ② gives $a = 2 \Rightarrow b = 3$

Coefficients

Multiplying out the brackets gives:

$$x^3 + ax^2 + bx + x^2 + ax + b \quad = x^3 + 3x^2 + 5x + 3$$
$$x^3 + (a + 1)x^2 + (a + b)x + b \quad = x^3 + 3x^2 + 5x + 3$$

If we want these to be equal for any value of x, they must be exactly the same. Equating the x^2 coefficients:

$$a + 1 = 3 \quad \Rightarrow a = 2$$

Equating the constant term:

$$b = 3$$

When we come to partial fractions later in this section, you will find that you need to use both of these methods: each is more convenient in certain situations. For the moment, here are a couple more examples, the first of which involves completing the square:

Example

Find the numbers m and n such that

$$5 + 4x - x^2 = m - (x - n)^2$$

for all real values of x.

Solution

$$m - (x - n)^2 \quad = \quad m - (x^2 - 2nx + n^2)$$
$$= \quad m - n^2 + 2nx - x^2$$

Comparing coefficients, $\quad 5 = m - n^2 \qquad \dots \text{①}$

$$\text{and} \quad 4 = 2n \qquad \dots \text{②}$$

From ②, $n = 2$; putting this into ① gives $5 = m - 4 \Rightarrow m = 9$.

Example

Given that $f(x) = x^4 + 2x^3 + x^2 - 28x - 60$, show that $f(x)$ may be expressed in the form $(x^2 + x + a)^2 - 4(x + b)^2$, where a and b are constants to be determined.

Solution

Since there are only two unknowns we normally only need two equations. Probably the easiest way, in order to avoid squaring a or b, is to equate x^2- and x-coefficients.

Squaring the first bracket gives: $x^2(2a + 1) + x(2a)$

The second bracket gives: $x^2(-4) + x(-8b)$

x^2-coeffs: $(2a + 1) + (-4) = 1$ $\Rightarrow 2a = 4$

                                     $\Rightarrow a = 2$

x-coeffs: $2a - 8b = -28$ $\Rightarrow 8b = 32$

                                        $b = 4$

You should now be able to answer Exercises 1, 2 and 3 on p. 14.

Fractions

We have already had some practice in adding and subtracting fractions: we're now going to look at some other operations involving fractions. You will probably find at some time that in your working of a problem you have an expression like:

a $\dfrac{1\frac{1}{2} + 2}{6}$ or   **b** $\dfrac{\frac{1}{x + 1} - 1}{x + 1}$ or   **c** $\dfrac{\frac{2}{x - 2} - \frac{2}{x + 2}}{x + 4}$

One of the easiest ways of making these a little neater is to multiply *every term* in the whole fraction by the offending denominator(s), i.e.:

a   multiply throughout by 2:

$$\frac{1\frac{1}{2} + 2}{6} = \frac{3 + 4}{12} = \frac{7}{12}$$

b   multiply throughout by $x + 1$:

$$\frac{\frac{1}{x + 1} - 1}{x + 1} = \frac{1 - (x + 1)}{(x + 1)^2} = \frac{1 - x - 1}{(x + 1)^2} = \frac{-x}{(x + 1)^2}$$

c   multiply throughout by $(x - 2)(x + 2)$:

$$\frac{\frac{2}{x - 2} - \frac{2}{x + 2}}{x + 4} = \frac{2(x + 2) - 2(x - 2)}{(x + 4)(x + 2)(x - 2)}$$

$$= \frac{2x + 4 - 2x + 4}{(x + 4)(x + 2)(x - 2)}$$

$$= \frac{8}{(x + 4)(x^2 - 4)}$$

You should now be able to answer Exercise 4 on p. 14.

Partial fractions

We're now going to work the other way round. Instead of learning how to combine fractions, we're going to see how we can split them into their components.

For example, we can combine the fractions $\frac{2}{x-1}$ and $\frac{3}{x-2}$:

$$\frac{2}{x-1} + \frac{3}{x-2} = \frac{(x-2) \times 2 + (x-1) \times 3}{(x-1)(x-2)}$$

$$= \frac{2x-4+3x-3}{(x-1)(x-2)}$$

$$= \frac{5x-7}{(x-1)(x-2)}$$

Working the other way round, if we have the fraction:

$$\frac{x+7}{(x-2)(x+1)}$$

can we find the two numbers A and B such that:

$$\frac{x+7}{(x-2)(x+1)} = \frac{A}{(x-2)} + \frac{B}{(x+1)}?$$

The method of finding these numbers is to put the two fractions together:

$$\frac{A}{(x-2)} + \frac{B}{(x+1)} = \frac{(x+1)A + (x-2)B}{(x-2)(x+1)}$$

and compare this with what we want, i.e.

$$\frac{(x+1)A + (x-2)B}{(x-2)(x+1)} = \frac{x+7}{(x-2)(x+1)}$$

We can see that the bottom lines are the same – we have to choose A and B so that the tops are also the same, i.e. so that:

$$(x+1)A + (x-2)B = x+7$$

This is to be true for any value of x, i.e. it is an *identity* and we can find the unknown constants by the methods we have already looked at earlier in this section. Let's rewrite it with the extra line in the equals sign:

$$(x+1)A + (x-2)B \equiv x+7$$

Since this is to be true for *any* value of x, we can substitute values that suit us. So we choose values that make the value of the brackets zero in turn, i.e.

putting $x = -1$: $(-1+1)A + (-1-2)B = -1+7$

$$-3B = 6$$

$$B = -2$$

putting $x = 2$: $3A = 9 \Rightarrow A = 3$

So our original fraction:

$$\frac{x + 7}{(x - 2)(x + 1)} \equiv \frac{3}{(x - 2)} - \frac{2}{(x + 1)}$$

which we can verify by recombining the fractions on the right-hand side. These two fractions are said to be the *partial fractions* of the original fraction.

Let's have a look at another example of this.

Example   Given that $f(x) \equiv \dfrac{1}{(1 + x)(1 - 2x)}$

express f(x) in partial fractions.

Solution   Let $\dfrac{1}{(1 + x)(1 - 2x)} \equiv \dfrac{A}{(1 + x)} + \dfrac{B}{(1 - 2x)}$

$$\equiv \frac{A(1 - 2x) + B(1 + x)}{(1 + x)(1 - 2x)}$$

Then   Putting $x = \frac{1}{2}$: $1 = \left(\frac{3}{2}\right)B \Rightarrow B = \frac{2}{3}$

Putting $x = -1$: $1 = 3A \Rightarrow A = \frac{1}{3}$

i.e. $f(x) \equiv \dfrac{1}{3(1 + x)} + \dfrac{2}{3(1 - 2x)}$

You should now be able to answer Exercise 5 on p. 14.

Quadratic factors

The next step is to look at the case when one of the factors in the denominator is quadratic, which means that the highest power of x occurring is two, something like $2x^2 + 3$ for example.

It could be that the quadratic factor can be factorised, e.g. $x^2 - 4$ could be expressed as $(x - 2)(x + 2)$, in which case all the factors are linear and the method above can be used. Otherwise, if the quadratic factor is *irreducible*, i.e. it cannot be put into real factors, we need to modify the method and use a different form of numerator (i.e. top of the fraction).

Let's take an example to see why this is so. Suppose we wanted to put the following function into partial fractions:

$$f(x) \equiv \frac{3x^2 + 3x + 2}{(x + 1)(x^2 + 1)}$$

If we suppose the two fractions are:

$$\frac{A}{x + 1} + \frac{B}{x^2 + 1}$$

we find that we need to choose A and B so that:

$$3x^2 + 3x + 2 \equiv A(x^2 + 1) + B(x + 1)$$

x^2-coeff: $3 = A$

x-coeff: $3 = B$

constant: $2 = A + B$

This last equation is not consistent with the other two, so we could never find suitable values for A and B. Instead, we suppose that the numerator of the quadratic factor is of the form $Bx + C$, i.e. put:

$$\frac{3x^2 + 3x + 2}{(x + 1)(x^2 + 1)} \equiv \frac{A}{x + 1} + \frac{Bx + C}{x^2 + 1}$$

$$\equiv \frac{A(x^2 + 1) + (Bx + C)(x + 1)}{(x + 1)(x^2 + 1)}$$

Then $3x^2 + 3x + 2 \equiv A(x^2 + 1) + (Bx + C)(x + 1)$

Put $x = -1$: $3 - 3 + 2 = 2A$

$$A = 1$$

There are no values of x that will make the bracket $(x^2 + 1)$ disappear, so to find B and C we use a different approach. Let's multiply the right-hand side out completely:

$$3x^2 + 3x + 2 \equiv Ax^2 + A + Bx^2 + Bx + Cx + C$$

$$\equiv (A + B)x^2 + (B + C)x + (A + C)$$

when we arrange the terms in descending powers of x. Now the fact that this is an identity means that *each* of the coefficients must be *identical on both sides*, i.e.:

x^2-coeff $3 = A + B$

x-coeff $3 = B + C$

constant $2 = A + C$

With the value of A we've already found, we now have:

$$A = 1, B = 2, C = 1$$

i.e. $$\frac{3x^2 + 3x + 2}{(x + 1)(x^2 + 1)} \equiv \frac{1}{x + 1} + \frac{2x + 1}{x^2 + 1}$$

In an actual question, we wouldn't write down the whole of the expansion of the right-hand side. As we did before, we would find the constant belonging with the linear factor (A in the last example) and then mentally find the coefficient of the x^2 term and the constant – these are usually the most straightforward to find. Let's work through an example of this.

Example Express $f(x) = \dfrac{x + 6}{(x + 1)(x^2 + 4)}$ in partial fractions.

Solution	Let	$\dfrac{x+6}{(x+1)\,(x^2+4)} \equiv \dfrac{A}{x+1} + \dfrac{Bx+C}{x^2+4}$

$$\equiv \frac{A(x^2+1) + (Bx+C)\,(x+1)}{(x+1)\,(x^2+4)}$$

i.e. $x + 6 \equiv A(x^2+4) + (Bx+C)\,(x+1)$ ... ①

Put $x = -1$: $5 = 5A$ $\Rightarrow A = 1$

(Now look on the right hand side of [1] for the coefficients of x^2; without multiplying out completely you can see that this is $A + B$. Similarly the constant must be $4A + C$. If you can't see this directly, then multiply out and collect together as we did in the previous example.)

Comparing coefficients of x^2 :

$$0 = A + B \Rightarrow B = -1$$

(The coefficient of x^2 on the left-hand side is 0 because there is no x^2 term.)

Comparing constants:

$$6 = 4A + C \Rightarrow C = 2$$

Then $\dfrac{x+6}{(x+1)\,(x^2+4)} \equiv \dfrac{1}{x+1} + \dfrac{2-x}{x^2+4}$

You should now be able to answer Exercise 6 on p. 14.

Repeated factors

There is one final type of fraction to look at: one of the factors on the bottom can be a 'repeated factor', something like $(x-2)^2$. Since this is a quadratic, we would expect to put $Ax + B$ on top as we did with the type above; instead we have the slightly curious procedure of putting:

$$\frac{A}{x-2} + \frac{B}{(x-2)^2}$$

Let's have a look at an example of this type. You'll notice that the gathering together of the *three* fractions is slightly more complicated.

Example	Express	$\dfrac{11-x-x^2}{(x+2)\,(x-1)^2}$ in partial fractions.

Solution	Let	$\dfrac{11-x-x^2}{(x+2)\,(x-1)^2} \equiv \dfrac{A}{x+2} + \dfrac{B}{x-1} + \dfrac{C}{(x-1)^2}$

$$\equiv \frac{A(x-1)^2 + B(x+2)\,(x-1) + C(x+2)}{(x+2)\,(x-1)^2}$$

7

You multiply the top by what isn't on the bottom, but *is* in the common denominator, i.e.:

$$11 - x - x^2 \equiv A(x-1)^2 + B(x+2)(x-1) + C(x+2)$$

At least with this type there are two values of x which make brackets disappear:

putting $x = 1$: $9 = 3C$ $\Rightarrow$ $C = 3$

putting $x = -2$: $9 = 9A$ $\Rightarrow$ $A = 1$

x^2-coeffs. : $-1 = A + B$ $\Rightarrow$ $B = -2$

i.e. $$\frac{11 - x - x^2}{(x+2)(x-1)^2} \equiv \frac{1}{x+2} - \frac{2}{x-1} + \frac{3}{(x-1)^2}$$

You should now be able to answer Exercise 7 on p. 14.

Dividing

One more point: if the highest power of x occurring on the top of the fraction is greater than or equal to the highest power on the bottom, *we have to divide through first of all* until the power on the bottom is greater than that on the top. The next section introduces this technique

Dividing polynomials

Before we can use our new methods for solving certain higher-order equations, the process covered next, there is a further technique which you will find useful, both here and in a number of other applications, which is a method for dividing polynomials.

Before we look at algebraic fractions, we'll run through a way of expressing a fraction like $\frac{645}{27}$ in the form $a + \frac{b}{27}$ where a and b are integers – you may already be familiar with it. The method of finding this is called 'long division'; it's set out like this:

$$27\overline{\smash{\big)}\,645}$$

Take the first two figures, 64, and find how many times 27 divides into them. This is 2, so write 2 above the second figure, 4:

$$\begin{array}{r} 2 \\ 27\overline{\smash{\big)}\,645} \end{array}$$

Then multiply 27 by the 2, put the result under the 64 and subtract:

$$\begin{array}{r} 2 \\ 27\overline{\smash{\big)}\,645} \\ 54 \\ \hline 10 \end{array}$$

Now bring down the next figure to join the 10:

$$\begin{array}{r} 2 \\ 27 \overline{)645} \\ 54 \\ \hline 105 \end{array}$$

and repeat the procedure, finding how many times 27 divides into 105. This is 3, so write the 3 next to the 2, multiply and subtract as before:

$$\begin{array}{r} 23 \\ 27 \overline{)645} \\ 54 \\ \hline 105 \\ 81 \\ \hline 24 \end{array}$$

This 24 is the remainder, and so finally we have:

$$\frac{645}{27} = 23\frac{24}{27}$$

It's worth knowing, and remembering this method, because to divide algebraically follows much the same pattern. Let's have a look at an example of this:

$$\frac{x^3 - 3x^2 + 2x + 7}{x + 1}$$

We'll set it out as for the arithmetic example:

$$x + 1 \overline{)x^3 - 3x^2 + 2x + 7}$$

The difference is that we only worry about the highest power of x in the numerator being divided and the highest power of x in the denominator doing the dividing, in the immediate case x^3 and x respectively. This gives x^2; now we proceed exactly as before:

$$\begin{array}{r} x^2 \\ x + 1 \overline{)x^3 - 3x^2 + 2x + 7} \\ x^3 + x^2 \\ \hline -4x^2 \end{array}$$

Remember that we *subtract* the $(x^3 + x^2)$ from $(x^3 - 3x^2)$. We can look on this as reversing the signs of $x^3 + x^2$, giving $-x^3 - x^2$, and *adding* this to $x^3 - 3x^2$, giving $-4x^2$ as we have already we bring the next term down and continue:

$$\begin{array}{r} x^2 - 4x + 6 \\ x + 1 \overline{\smash{\big)}\ x^3 - 3x^2 + 2x + 7} \\ \underline{x^3 + x^2} \\ -4x^2 + 2x \\ \underline{-4x^2 - 4x} \\ 6x + 7 \\ \underline{6x + 6} \\ 1 \end{array}$$

The remainder is 1, so:

$$\frac{x^3 - 3x^2 + 2x + 7}{x + 1} = x^2 - 4x + 6 + \frac{1}{x + 1}$$

You should now be able to answer Exercise 8 on p. 14.

The remainder and factor theorems

We already know that we can solve any quadratic equation by putting the coefficients into a formula. If there are powers of x higher than two in an equation, for example

$$x^4 - x^3 + 7x + 6 = 0,$$

there is no equivalent formula and we have to use other methods. In this section we are going to look at two theorems which can help us solve equations like these, especially if at least some of the roots are integers.

The remainder theorem

Suppose we had the polynomial:

$$P(x) \quad = \quad x^3 - 3x^2 + 5x - 3$$

If we divided this by $(x - 2)$, what remainder would we be left with? We could find out by long division:

$$\begin{array}{r} x^2 - x + 3 \\ x - 2 \overline{\smash{\big)}\ x^3 - 3x^2 + 5x - 3} \\ \underline{x^3 - 2x^2} \\ -x^2 + 5x \\ \underline{-x^2 + 2x} \\ 3x - 3 \\ \underline{3x - 6} \\ 3 \end{array}$$

So the remainder is 3, with a quotient of $x^2 - x + 3$. Now you have a go, dividing the same polynomial $P(x)$ by $(x + 2)$.

You should have ended up with a remainder of –33 and a quotient of $x^2 - 5x + 15$. (If not, check that you have taken each line away correctly from the one above.)

There is a quicker way of finding the remainder. If we do not need to know the quotient we use the *remainder theorem*.

Remainder theorem

If a polynomial P(x) is divided by (x – a)

then the remainder is P(a)

Let's check this with the remainders we have already found:

When we divide P(x) by $(x - 2)$, $a = 2$ and
$$P(2) = 8 - 3 \times 4 + 5 \times 2 - 3 = 3$$
With the one you tried, $(x + 2)$, $a = -2$ and
$$P(-2) = -8 - 3 \times 4 + 5\,(-2) - 3 = -33$$
So it works with those two. Can we see why it works? Using the results from our divisions, we could write:
$$P(x) = (x - 2)\,(x^2 - x + 3) + 3$$
and $$P(x) = (x + 2)\,(x^2 - 5x + 15) - 33$$
In fact, if we divide P(x) by $(x - a)$, where a is any number, we will get a quotient, which we can call Q (x), and a remainder R. We could write:
$$P(x) \equiv (x - a)\,Q(x) + R$$
If we substitute $x = a$ on both sides of this identity, the bracket $(x - a)$ is zero and we have:
$$P(a) = 0 \times Q(a) + R = R$$
and this is what the remainder theorem states.

Example	What is the remainder when $x^4 - 3\,x^3 + x - 6$ is divided by
	a $(x - 3)$ **b** $(x + 2)$?

Solution	Let $P(x) \equiv x^4 - 3\,x^3 + x - 6$.
	a Here $a = 3$, so by the remainder theorem the remainder is:
	$P(3) = 81 - 81 + 3 - 6 = -3$
	b Here $a = -2$, so the remainder is $P(-2) = 16 + 24 - 2 - 6 = 32$

The factor theorem

If we have a polynomial, $P(x)$, and we want to solve the equation $P(x) = 0$, we need to find the factors of $P(x)$. Of course, if dividing by $(x - a)$ leaves a remainder, $(x - a)$ cannot be a factor. On the other hand, if the remainder is zero, it means that $(x - a)$ *is* a factor ...

Factor theorem

If, for any polynomial P(x), P(a) = 0,

then (x – a) is a factor.

Let's take the polynomial $P(x) = x^3 - 2x^2 - 5x + 6$. We want to find values of x such that $P(x) = 0$.

$$
\begin{array}{lll}
P(1) = & 1 - 2 - 5 + 6 & = 0 & \text{so } (x - 1) \text{ is a factor} \\
P(-1) = & -1 - 2 + 5 + 6 & = 8 & \text{so } (x + 1) \text{ is not a factor} \\
P(2) = & 8 - 8 - 10 + 6 & = -4 & \text{so } (x - 2) \text{ is not a factor} \\
P(-2) = & -8 - 8 + 10 + 6 & = 0 & \text{so } (x + 2) \text{ is a factor} \\
P(3) = & 27 - 18 - 15 + 6 & = 0 & \text{so } (x - 3) \text{ is a factor} \\
\text{so } P(x) = & x^3 - 2x^2 - 5x + 6 & = (x - 1)(x + 2)(x - 3)
\end{array}
$$

Note:

1 We look at the highest power of x in the polynomial, in this case 3, then we know that there are at most 3 factors.

2 We look at the constant term, in this case + 6, then we need only try values of x that are factors of 6, i.e.

$\pm 1, \pm 2, \pm 3, \pm 6$.

They are not always that easy. Sometimes only some of the roots are integers. The other roots may be fractions, which makes them harder to spot, or irrationals, or there may be no further real roots. Suppose, for example, that we have found a polynomial $P(x)$ to have as factors $(x - 1)$ and:

● $(2x^2 - x - 1)$: this factorises to $(2x + 1)(x - 1)$, so $P(-\frac{1}{2})$ is in fact zero but we could not be expected to discover this by ourselves at the outset

● $(2x^2 + x - 1)$: this has real factors but they are irrational (to find the roots of the equation $P(x) = 0$ we would have to use the quadratic formula)

● $(2x^2 + x + 1)$: this has no real factors.

Further examples

Now here are a couple more examples of different kinds that crop up in exam papers.

Example

If $P(x) = x^3 - Kx^2 + 3x + 5$ leaves a remainder of 3 when divided by $(x - 2)$, find K.

Solution

$P(2) = 8 - 4K + 6 + 5 = 3$ by remainder theorem.

$$\Rightarrow 19 - 4K = 3, \text{ so } K = 4$$

Example

The polynomial $2x^3 - 3ax^2 + ax + b$ has a factor of $(x - 1)$ and, when divided by $(x - 2)$, a remainder of -54 is obtained. Find the values of a and b and factorise the polynomial.

Solution

Put $P(x) = 2x^3 - 3ax^2 + ax + b$

If $(x - 1)$ is a factor, then $P(1) = 0$.

$$P(1) = 2 - 3a + a + b = 0$$
$$b - 2a = -2 \qquad \qquad \dots ①$$

Also $P(-2) = -54$ by remainder theorem

$$P(-2) = -16 - 12a - 2a + b = -54$$
$$b - 14a = -38 \qquad \qquad \dots ②$$

Solving ① and ② simultaneously, $a = 3$ and $b = 4$

Then $P(x) = 2x^3 - 9x^2 + 3x + 4$

Divide this by the factor $(x - 1)$

$$
\begin{array}{r}
2x^2 - 7x - 4 \\
x - 1 \overline{\smash{\big)}\ 2x^3 - 9x^2 + 3x + 4} \\
\underline{2x^3 - 2x^2} \\
-7x^2 + 3x \\
\underline{-7x^2 + 7x} \\
-4x + 4 \\
\underline{-4x + 4}
\end{array}
$$

$$P(x) = (x - 1)(2x^2 - 7x - 4)$$
$$= (x - 1)(2x + 1)(x - 4)$$

Note: If the question says factorise completely, the factors will usually all be linear.

You should now be able to answer Exercises 9 to 15 on p. 15.

EXERCISES

1 Find the values of p, q and r such that:

$$p(x + q)^2 + r = 4x^2 - 6x + 5$$

for all values of x

2 Find the values of the positive constants a, b and c such that:

$$a - (bx + c)^2 = 2 - 4x - 4x^2$$

for all values of x.

3 The constants m, n, p and q are chosen so that the identity:

$$(mt + n)(t^2 - 4t + 5) \equiv 2t^3 + pt^2 + qt + 5$$

is true for all values of t. find the values of m, n, p and q.

4 Simplify the following fractions:

a $\dfrac{1 + \dfrac{2}{x}}{\dfrac{2}{x} - 1}$ **b** $\dfrac{1 - \dfrac{y^2}{x^2}}{1 + \dfrac{y^2}{x^2}}$ **c** $\dfrac{x - \dfrac{1}{x}}{1 + \dfrac{1}{x}}$ **d** $\dfrac{2}{1 - x^2} + \left(\dfrac{1}{1 - x} - \dfrac{1}{1 + x}\right)$

[sort out the bracket first]

e $\dfrac{\dfrac{2}{1 + x} - \dfrac{1}{1 - x}}{1 + x^2}$ **f** $\dfrac{(2x + 1)^2}{2x^2 - \dfrac{1}{2}}$

5 Put the following functions into partial fractions:

a $\dfrac{2x + 10}{(x - 1)(x + 2)}$ **b** $\dfrac{7}{(-2x)(4 - x)}$ **c** $\dfrac{2x}{x^2 - 1}$

6 Express the following functions in partial fractions:

a $\dfrac{3x^2}{(x - 2)(x^2 + 2)}$ **b** $\dfrac{x^2 - 2x + 5}{(x - 1)(x^2 + 1)}$ **c** $\dfrac{8 - 3x}{(x + 4)(x^2 + 4)}$

7 Express in partial fractions:

a $\dfrac{4 + 5x - x^2}{(x - 1)(x + 1)^2}$ **b** $\dfrac{4x^2 - 12x - 15}{(x + 2)(x - 3)^2}$ **c** $\dfrac{x^2 + 1}{(x + 1)(x + 2)}$

8 Divide the following:

a $\dfrac{2x^2 - 7x - 1}{x - 3}$ **b** $\dfrac{x^3 - 6x^2 + 11x - 6}{x - 1}$

c $\dfrac{x^3 - 5x^2 - 2x + 24}{x + 2}$ **d** $\dfrac{6x^3 + 7x^2 - x - 2}{2x - 1}$

9 What is the remainder when $x^4 + 2x^3 - x^2 + x - 4$ is divided by $(x - 2)$?

10 What is the remainder when $x^3 - 3x^2 - 4x + 7$ is divided by $(x + 2)$?

11 Factorise completely: $x^3 - x^2 - 9x + 9$

12 Put into linear factors: $x^3 + 3x^2 - 13x - 15$

13 Factorise into one linear and one quadratic factor: $x^3 + 3x^2 - 8x - 4$

14 When the polynomial $f(x) = x^3 + ax^2 + bx - 10$ is divided by $(x + 1)$ and $(x - 1)$ the remainders are -6 and -10 respectively. Find the values of a and b.

15 If $Q(x) = x^4 + hx^3 + gx^2 - 16x - 12$ has factors $(x + 1)$ and $(x - 2)$ find the constants h and g and the remaining factors.

SUMMARY

It is very important that you are able to perform these basic algebraic techniques accurately. You will find this ability pays handsome dividends as you progress through the course.

2.

Logarithms and Exponentials

INTRODUCTION   We shall continue the work from the previous module on logarithms and start to investigate their properties – this will enable us to solve a different type of equation, involving unknown powers, and also lay the foundation for the kind of manipulation that you will need later in the course.

Logarithms

Having used the × sign to express the operation of *adding*, for instance, four 3's together,

$$3 \times 4 = 12,$$

we use the ÷ sign for the *inverse* of this operation. In other words, given the result 12, how many 3's did we start with to give this sum? We would write this, together with the answer, as:

$$12 \div 3 = 4$$

A very similar relationship holds between indices and logarithms (or *logs* for short). *Indices* express the operation of *multiplying*, for instance, four 3's together

$$3^4 = 81$$

and logs ask the question – how many 3's multiplied together give 81? This is written

$$\log_3 81 = 4$$

and the number that we're multiplying together, 3 in this case, is called the *base* of the logarithm.

If we take another example, $\log_2 32$ asks the question: 'How many 2s do I need to multiply together to give 32?' The answer here would be 5, since we know that $2^5 = 32$.

You should be able to answer Exercise 1 on p. 24 at this point.

Taking these last two examples, we can see that the statement $3^4 = 81$ is equivalent to the statement $\log_3 81 = 4$, and the statement $2^5 = 32 \Leftrightarrow \log_2 32 = 5$. In general, we have:

$$a^b = c \Leftrightarrow \log_a c = b$$

where the $\Leftrightarrow$ sign means that either of the two statements imply the other.

We can use these equivalent forms to derive a very important property of logarithms. Suppose we had the positive numbers e and f, with $e = a^p$ and $f = a^q$, where a is a positive constant. We can rewrite these last two statements as:

$$\log_a e = p \quad \text{and} \quad \log_a f = q \qquad ①$$

Now $e \times f = a^p \times a^q = a^{p+q}$ and writing this in logarithm form:

$$\log_a e \times f \ = p + q$$
$$= \log_a e + \log_a f \quad \text{from } ①$$

The result, $\log_a ef = \log_a e + \log_a f$, is true for any two positive numbers e and f and any suitable base a. To show that the result is true for any base, we write simply log, without a base, so that:

Property 1

$$\log ab = \log a + \log b$$

If we put $a = b$ into this result, we have:

$$\log a^2 = \log a + \log a = 2 \log a$$

and the same applies for any number of a's, leading to an important result:

Property 2

$$\log a^n = n \log a$$

So, for example,

$$\log_2 (8)^{10} \ = \ 10 \log_2 8$$
$$= \ 10 \times 3 = 30$$

You should now be able to answer Exercise 2 on p. 24.

Fractions

The examples up to now have been reasonably straightforward, with all the powers involved being integers. In fact, exactly the same relationship holds for any kind of index – fractional, negative or decimal. Let's have a look at some examples of this written in each of the equivalent forms:

$$9^{\frac{1}{2}} = 3 \qquad \log_9 3 = \frac{1}{2}$$

$$5^{-1} = \frac{1}{5} \qquad \log_5 \frac{1}{5} = -1$$

$$16^{0.75} = 8 \qquad \log_{16} 8 = 0.75$$

To make our definition of log a little more meaningful, we can now look at it as asking the question 'What power of the *base* gives me such and such a number?'

what power of this number, gives me this?

and the answer in this case would be $\frac{1}{3}$, since $8^{\frac{1}{3}} = 2$.

We can use our knowledge of indices to derive a further useful property.

$$\log_a \left(\frac{1}{b}\right) = \log_a (b^{-1}) \qquad \text{definition of negative powers}$$

$$= -\log_a b \qquad \text{from Property 2}$$

So, for example,

$$\log_2 \left(\frac{1}{4}\right) = \log_2 (4^{-1})$$

$$= -\log_2 4 = -2$$

Property 3	$$\log \frac{1}{b} = -\log b$$

We can combine properties 1 and 3 to show another property:

Property 4	$$\log a - \log b = \log a + \log \frac{1}{b} = \log \frac{a}{b}$$

Two particular logs are worth noting. From our work on indices, we know that if a is any number, $a^0 = 1$ and $a^1 = a$.

In log form, this is

Property 5	$\log_a 1 = 0 \text{ and } \log_a a = 1$

We can use these properties to simplify expressions containing logs – these will start to crop up with increasing frequency as we continue – and also to solve equations involving logs. Let's have a look at an example of each of these.

Example   Express $\log 8 - \log 6 + \log 3$ as a multiple of $\log 2$.

Solution

$$\log 8 - \log 6 + \log 3 \;=\; \log \tfrac{8}{6} + \log 3$$

$$=\; \log \tfrac{8 \times 3}{6} \;=\; \log 4 \;=\; \log 2^2$$

$$=\; 2 \log 2$$

Example   Given that:

$$1 + \log_a (7x - 3a) = 2 \log_a x + \log_a 2,$$

find, in terms of a, the possible values of x.

Solution   When there are mixtures of logs and ordinary numbers, we collect all the terms containing logs to one side and all the rest of the terms to the other (as a general rule). This will give:

$$1 = 2 \log_a x + \log_a 2 - \log_a (7x - 3a)$$

Now we can start reducing all these terms on the RHS to one term by using the properties of logs:

$$
\begin{aligned}
1 \;&=\; \log_a x^2 + \log_a 2 - \log_a (7x - 3a) && \text{Property 2} \\
&=\; \log_a 2x^2 - \log_a (7x - 3a) && \text{Property 1} \\
&=\; \log_a \frac{2x^2}{7x - 3a} && \text{Property 4}
\end{aligned}
$$

Putting this into the equivalent expression involving indices:

$$\frac{2x^2}{7x - 3a} \;=\; a^1 \;=\; a$$

$$\Rightarrow \quad 2x^2 = 7ax - 3a^2$$

$$\text{i.e.} \quad 2x^2 - 7ax + 3a^2 = 0$$

$$(2x - a)(x - 3a) = 0$$

$$x = \frac{a}{2} \quad \text{or} \quad x = 3a$$

Before we proceed any further, let's make a table to summarise the results we've found so far:

$$a^b = c \quad \Leftrightarrow \quad \log_a c = b$$

$$\log a + \log b = \log ab$$

$$\log a - \log b = \log \frac{a}{b}$$

$$\log a^n = n \log a$$

$$\log \frac{1}{a} = -\log a$$

$$\log 1 = 0$$

You should now be able to answer Exercises 3, 4, 5 and 6 on pp. 24–25.

Two common bases

So far we've been working with the properties of logs and using these to put various combinations into different forms. These properties are true for any log, regardless of the base to which they have been taken. When we come to mix logs with ordinary numbers, we find that different bases give different values, e.g.:

$$\log_2 6 = 2.585$$
$$\log_3 6 = 1.631$$
$$\log_6 6 = 1$$
$$\log_{10} 6 = 0.778 \text{ (each to 3 d.p.)}$$

For convenience, two particular bases have been chosen as standard – each of them has properties which make it useful for certain situations.

One of these bases is written e. In value, $e \approx 2.7182818$. Logarithms taken to this base are called *natural* logarithms (at the moment this may seem a rather unlikely title) and are written $\log_e$ or 'ln' for short. In most of our work we shall be using this type of log.

The other base that is commonly used, base 10, ties in very well with our usual number system, which as you probably know is also to the base 10. In the days when calculations had to be done by hand, before the appearance of electronic calculators, logs to this base were by far the most convenient – nowadays they are used less and it's quite possible that you'll never see them mentioned in a question. They are written $\log_{10}$ or 'lg' for short ('log' on some calculators).

Have a look at your calculator – can you see the two different function buttons LN and LOG, with inverse functions e^x and 10^x respectively? You will certainly have LN but if there is no LOG button it shouldn't be a problem. The relationshp between e^x and ln is important.

$$y = e^x \Leftrightarrow x = \ln y$$

So that, for example, if $e^x = 4$ then $x = \ln 4$

and if $\ln y = x - 2$, then $y = e^{x-2}$

Let's see how we can use the properties of logs and our calculators to solve a certain type of equation.

Equations with variable indices

How can we find the value of x which makes the following equation true?

$$3^x = 25$$

It's possible by means of trial and error with the x^y (or equivalent) function on a calculator. You may like to have a go at this – how close to 25 can you make 3^x by trying suitable values of x?

How did you get on? After some time you may have managed to produce something that was pretty close – taking x to be 2.929947 gave 3^x as 24.999999, but it took quite a lot of experimentation. Fortunately, there is an easier way. If the two sides of the equation are equal, then log of one side must be equal to the log of the other. Taking logs of both sides,

$$\log (3^x) = \log 25,$$

and using Property 2 of logs, $\log (a^n) = n \log a$, we can rewrite this as:

$$x \log 3 = \log 25$$

so $$x = \frac{\log 25}{\log 3}$$

You can try using both lg ($\log_{10}$) and ln ($\log_e$) to evaluate this fraction – they should both give the same answer.

As you can see, it doesn't matter to what base the logs are taken – the ratio:

$$\frac{\log 25}{\log 3}$$

turns out to be approximately 2.929947, the value found using the long method of trial and error. Let's have a look at one more example of this.

| **Example** | Find the least integer p such that 1.5^p has a value greater than a million. |

| **Solution** | First of all, we'll find the approximate value of p for *equality*, i.e. that |

$$1.5^p = 1,000,000$$

Taking logs to the base e of both sides,

$$\ln(1.5^p) = \ln 1,000,000$$
$$p \ln(1.5) = \ln 1,000,000$$
$$p = \frac{\ln 1,000,000}{\ln 1.5} = 34.07$$

If p has to be a whole number and 1.5^p has to be *greater* than a million, we have to round up, so $p = 35$

We can check this: 1.5^{34} is less than a million

1.5^{35} is more than a million.

You should now be able to answer Exercises 7 and 8 on p. 25.

Further examples

We can use the same method for slightly more complicated examples where there are two numbers, each having a variable power. Let's try one of these.

| **Example** | Solve the equation $3^{2x+1} = 4^{x-1}$, giving three significant figures in your answer. |

| **Solution** | Taking logs to the base e of both sides, |

$$\ln(3^{2x+1}) = \ln(4^{x-1})$$

using index property: $(2x+1)\ln 3 = (x-1)\ln 4$

multiplying out: $2x \ln 3 + \ln 3 = x \ln 4 - \ln 4$

x's to one side: $\ln 3 + \ln 4 = x \ln 4 - 2x \ln 3$

factorising: $\ln 3 + \ln 4 = x(\ln 4 - 2\ln 3)$

and so $x = \frac{\ln 3 + \ln 4}{\ln 4 - 2\ln 3} = -3.06$ (to 3 sig figs)

Before you use this method, just check that the two base numbers are not closely related:

$$2^{2x+1} = 8^{x-1}$$

can be solved more quickly by putting $8 = 2^3$. This changes the equation to:

$$2^{2x+1} = (2^3)^{x-1} = 2^{3(x-1)}$$

Since the powers are of the same base, they must be equal, i.e.

$$2x + 1 = 3(x - 1) = 3x - 3 \Rightarrow x = 4$$

Exponential growth and decay

When the rate of change of a variable with respect to time is proportional to the amount of the variable present, the change is said to be *exponential*. If the variable is written as x, then both the equations

$$\frac{dx}{dt} = kx \quad \text{or} \quad \frac{dx}{dt} = -kx,$$

where t is a positive constant, representing exponential change. We shall see later that these equations have solutions

$$x = Ae^{kt} \quad \text{and} \quad x = Ae^{-kt}, \text{ where } A \text{ is a constant.}$$

If x_0 is the initial value of x (i.e. when $t = 0$) and we substitute these values into the equations, we find that

$$x_0 = Ae^0 = A$$

and the equations become

$$x = x_0 e^{kt} \quad \text{and} \quad x = x_0 e^{-kt}$$

Let's have a look at a couple of examples: in the first we are told the value of x_0 and of k and we have to find the time corresponding to a new value of x.

Example

The current, I amps, flowing through an electrical circuit at time t seconds is known to be decreasing according to the equation

$$I = I_0 e^{-5t}$$

where I_0 is the current initially flowing.

Given that the initial current in this circuit is 2 amps, calculate how long it takes for the current to decrease to 0.5 amps, giving your answer in seconds correct to two decimal places.

Solution

Given that $I_0 = 2$, we can rewrite the given equation as:

$$I = 2e^{-5t}$$

Now when $I = 0.5,$ $\quad 0.5 = 2e^{-5t}$

$$0.25 = e^{-5t} = \frac{1}{e^{5t}} \quad \Leftrightarrow \quad e^{5t} = \frac{1}{0.25} = 4$$

$$5t = \ln 4 \quad \Rightarrow t = \frac{1}{5} \ln 4 = 0.28 \text{ seconds (2 d.p.)}$$

In the second example, we are given an extra pair of values for the variables: with this, we can calculate the value of the unknown k.

Example   The variable x satisfies the equation:

$$x = x_0 e^{-kt}$$

If the value of x was 20 initially and it decreases to 10 when $t = 2$, find the value of k to two decimal places. Hence find the further time required for x to decrease to 8.

Solution   We're given that $x_0 = 20$, so that

$$x = 20e^{-kt}$$

Substituting the values $x = 10$ when $t = 2$,

$$10 = 20e^{-2k} \Rightarrow \frac{1}{2} = e^{-2k} = \frac{1}{e^{2k}} \Rightarrow e^{2k} = 2 \qquad \text{i.e. } 2k = \ln 2$$

$$\Rightarrow k = \frac{1}{2}\ln 2$$

$$\Rightarrow k = 0.35 \ (2 \text{ d.p.})$$

so $x = 20e^{-0.35t}$

When $x = 8$, $8 = 20e^{-0.35t}$

$$0.4 = e^{-0.35t} = \frac{1}{e^{0.35t}} \Rightarrow e^{0.35t} = \frac{1}{0.4} = \frac{5}{2}$$

$$\Rightarrow 0.35t = \ln\frac{5}{2}$$

$$\Rightarrow t = \frac{1}{0.35} \times \ln\frac{5}{2} = 2.6$$

Since t was 2 when x was 10, the further time e is $2.6 - 2 = 0.6$ (1 d.p.)

You should now be able to answer Exercise 9, 10, 11 and 12 on p. 25.

EXERCISES

1 Evaluate:

    a $\log 4$ **b** $\log_3 27$ **c** $\log_5 25$

    d $\log_8 8$ **e** $\log_{10} 10{,}000$ **f** $\log_a a^5$

2 Evaluate:

    a $\log_4 (16 \times 64)$ **b** $\log_2 (16 \times 64)$ **c** $\log_2 (64)^5$ **d** $\log_a (a^7)^3$

3 Evaluate:

    a $\log_4 2$ **b** $\log_3 \frac{1}{3}$ **c** $\log_{10} 0.01$ **d** $\log_8 4$ **e** $\log_4 32$ **f** $\log_p (p^{-4})$

4 Express as a multiple of log 2:

    a $\log 16 - \log 10 - \log 4 + \log 20$ **b** $3 \log 3 + 2 \log 4 - 3 \log 6 - \log 8$

5 Express as a single log:

    a $\log xy + 2 \log x - 3 \log y$ **b** $2 \log p - 2 \log q + \log p^2 q + \log pq^2$

6 Solve the equations:

    a $\log_x 4 = \dfrac{1}{2}$ **b** $2 + \log_2 x = 2 \log_2 (x + 1)$

    c $3^{2x} - 5(3^x) + 6 = 0$, by putting $y = 3^x$ **d** $\lg x + \lg (3x + 1) = 1$

7 Solve: **a** $2^x = 4{,}000$ **b** $3^{y + 2} = 250$

    In each case give your answer correct to two decimal places.

8 Find the least value of the integer n for which $(0.9)^n < 0.001$.

9 Find x to three significant figures, given that:

    $5^{2x} = 8^{x + 1}$

10 Solve the following equations:

    a $9^{2x - 3} = 3^{3x + 1}$ (Hint: express both as powers of 3)

    b $4^{2x + 1} = 8^{x - 1}$ (Hint: express both as powers of 2)

11 The total number of people, n, who have contacted a new advice centre t weeks after its opening is modelled by:

    $n = 6e^{0.3(t-1)}$, where $1 \le t \le 10$.

    a Calculate n when $t = 1$.

    b Calculate the value of t when the total number of people contacting the centre has risen to 49, giving your answer to the nearest whole number.

12 The number, N, of radioactive atoms present at time t seconds when a particular element decays is given by the equation $N = 10^{26} e^{-2t}$.

    a State the number of radioactive atoms initially present.

    b Sketch the graph of N against t.

    c Calculate how long it takes for the number of radioactive atoms present to be reduced to half the number initially present.

SUMMARY

We have been dealing with functions which are very important for our studies because they figure in the solution of naturally occurring problems. You need to make sure you are confident of combining logs by use of the appropriate rules.

3

Straight lines

INTRODUCTION
The advantage of straight lines is that we can plot them quite easily and accurately and use these graphs to predict other points. This property is exploited in this section where we will transform quite complicated equations into straight line equations and from these work out various values. We shall start, however, by extending the theory of straight lines that we started in the previous module.

Perpendicular and parallel lines

You will remember from Module P1 that if two lines, $y = m_1 x + c_1$ and $y = m_2 x + c_2$, are parallel, they have the same *gradient*, i.e. $m_1 = m_2$.

Figure 3.1

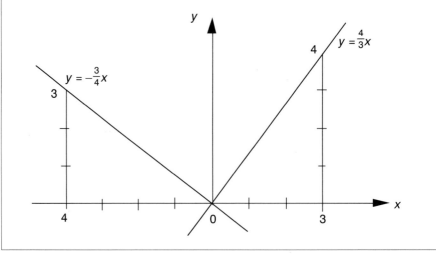

If we look at a part of the lines $y = \frac{4}{3}x$ and $y = -\frac{3}{4}x$ we can see that they are perpendicular to each other. While the line $y = \frac{4}{3}x$ goes along 3, it goes *up* 4. The line $y = -\frac{3}{4}x$ does just the opposite. As it goes along 4, it goes *down* 3.

The gradients of these lines are respectively $\frac{4}{3}$ and $-\frac{3}{4} = -\frac{1}{\frac{4}{3}}$. This is true for any two perpendicular lines: if the gradient of one is m, the gradient of the other, m' say, is $\frac{-1}{m}$ i.e. $m' = \frac{-1}{m} \Rightarrow mm' = -1$.

This is a very important result and is summarised below.

> If two lines have gradients m_1 and m_2 then
>
> **a** $\quad m_1 = m_2 \quad \Leftrightarrow \quad$ lines are parallel
>
> **b** $\quad m_1 m_2 = -1 \quad \Leftrightarrow \quad$ lines are perpendicular

Example

a Show that the lines $y = 4x - 3$ and $x + 4y - 8 = 0$ are perpendicular.

b Find a line perpendicular to the line $3x + 4y - 5 = 0$.

Solutions

a The first equation is in the form $y = mx + c$ and we can read off the gradient m as 4.

After rearranging, the second equation is $y = -\frac{1}{4}x + 2$ and so the gradient is $-\frac{1}{4}$.

$4 \times -\frac{1}{4} = -1$, so the lines are perpendicular.

Rearranging to $y = -\frac{3}{4}x + \frac{5}{4}$, we can see that

b The gradient of $3x + 4y - 5 = 0$ is $-\frac{3}{4}$, so we want the gradient of the other line, m say, to be such that

$$\left(-\frac{3}{4}\right) \times m = -1 \quad \Rightarrow \quad m = \frac{4}{3}$$

So any line with a gradient of $\frac{4}{3}$ would be perpendicular, for instance:

$$y = \frac{4}{3}x - 1 \quad \text{or, clearing fractions,} \quad 3y = 4x - 3$$

Example

Find the equation of the line joining $A(-1, -9)$ to $B(6, 12)$.

Another line passes through $C(7, -5)$ and meets AB at right angles at D. Find the equation of CD and calculate the coordinates of D.

Solution   The gradient of the line joining these points is:

$$\frac{12-(-9)}{6-(-1)} = \frac{21}{7} = 3.$$

A convenient formula for finding the equation of a line with gradient m, passing through the point (x_1, y_1), is

$$y - y_1 = m(x - x_1)$$

In this case, $m = 3$ and we can take either point as (x_1, y_1) say $A(-1, -9)$. Then the required equation is:

$$y - (-9) = 3(x - (-1)) \Rightarrow y + 9 = 3x + 3 \qquad \text{i.e. } y = 3x - 6$$

Figure 3.2

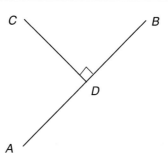

The gradient of AB is 3, so the equation of the line CD, perpendicular to AB, is $-\frac{1}{3}$. Passing through $C(7, -5)$, it has equation, using the formula above,

$$y - (-5) = -\frac{1}{3}(x - 7) \Rightarrow y + 5 = -\frac{1}{3}x + \frac{7}{3}$$

i.e. $3y + 15 = -x + 7 \Rightarrow 3y + x + 8 = 0$

We need the intersection of the two lines. Putting $y = 3x - 6$ into the equation we have just found gives $3(3x - 6) + x + 8 = 0$

$$\Rightarrow 9x - 18 + x + 8 = 0 \Rightarrow 10x = 10$$

$$\Rightarrow x = 1 \text{ and } y = -3.$$

The coordinates of D are $(1, -3)$.

You should now be able to answer Exercise 1 on p. 32.

Mid-points

To find the mid-point of the line joining two points, we take the *average* of the x-coordinates and the average of the y-coordinates. For example, the mid-point of the line joining the points $(-1, 4)$ and $(7, -2)$ would be

$$\left(\frac{-1 + 7}{2}, \frac{4 + (-2)}{2}\right)$$

i.e. $(3, 1)$.

(A common mistake here, by the way is to *subtract* the x and y-coordinates.)

You should now be able to answer Exercise 2 on p. 32.

We shall now proceed to a topic which has many practical applications: fitting a suitable equation to data collected from an experiment.

Linear form

When carrying out experiments to investigate the relationship between two variables, the *type* of equation linking the two can be known although the precise details are still unknown. In this section we're going to see how the equation can be transformed so that the results of the experiment can be used to calculate the unknown constants of the equation.

Two related variables

Suppose we have carried out an experiment to see how a variable y changes as we change another variable x, and have collected the following results:

x	1	2	3	4	5	6	cm (exact)
y	0.50	0.85	1.12	1.34	1.50	1.63	cm (2 d.p.)

x and y are known to be related by the equation:

$$\frac{a}{x} + \frac{b}{y} = 1$$

and we want to estimate values for the constants a and b using these data.

The method is to change the variables of the relating equation so that the new equation will be in the form of a straight line $Y = mX + c$.

In the above example, if we put $Y = \dfrac{1}{y}$ and $X = \dfrac{1}{x}$ the given equation becomes:

$$aX + bY = 1 \quad \Rightarrow bY = -aX + 1$$

$$\Rightarrow Y = \frac{-a}{b}X + \frac{1}{b}$$

29

So if we plot $\frac{1}{y}$ against $\frac{1}{x}$, the resulting points should lie more or less on a straight line with gradient $-\frac{a}{b}$ and y-intercept $\frac{1}{b}$. From these, we can calculate estimates for a and b.

Let's try this, making a table to include the new variables.

x	1	2	3	4	5	6
y	0.50	0.85	1.12	1.34	1.50	1.63
$X = \dfrac{1}{x}$	1	0.50	0.33	0.25	0.20	0.17
$Y = \dfrac{1}{y}$	2	1.18	0.89	0.75	0.67	0.61

We look at the range of values of the variables before choosing the scales so that the graph is a reasonable size. Here X is between 0 and 1, Y between 0 and 2 so we can take 1 cm for 0.2 on the X-axis and 1 cm for 0.4 on the Y-axis.

Figure 3.3

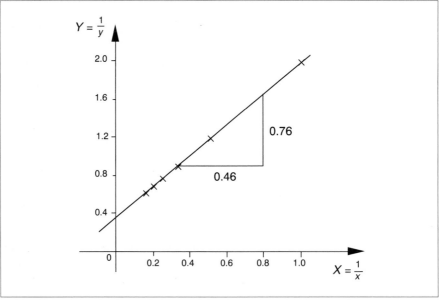

We plot the points and draw a line that fits these points as best we can: we do not expect a perfect straight line. From this line we calculate the gradient and find the y-intercept.

We can read the y-intercept straight off: it is about 0.36. Since this is $\frac{1}{b}$, our estimate of b is $\frac{1}{0.36}$ = 2.8 (1 d.p.)

The gradient is approximately $\dfrac{0.76}{0.46} = 1.65$. This is $-\dfrac{a}{b}$.

So $\qquad a \approx -b \times 1.65 \approx -4.6 \quad (1 \text{ d.p.})$

You can see that this method of transforming curves to straight lines is fairly effective. Not only do you find immediate confirmation that the relationship is as you supposed (or otherwise if the points are *not* on a straight line), but you can quickly work out an estimate for the actual function.

Different types

We can look now at ways of reducing other types of relationship to the form of a straight line, something like:

$$Y = aX + b$$

where Y and X are the new variables, a and b are constants to be found.

This can be very straightforward in certain cases – if the variables are connected by:

$$y^2 = ax + b$$

for example, all we need to do is set $Y = y^2$ and plotting Y against x should give a straight line from which we can calculate a and b.

In other cases there may not be a constant term in the relation, like $y = ax + \dfrac{b}{x}$. In a situation like this, we multiply or divide by something which leaves one of the terms constant, e.g. in this example we multiply by x. This gives $xy = ax^2 + b$ and so our straight line equation could come from setting $Y = xy$ and $X = x^2$. Conversely, given an equation like $y = ax^2 + bx$, we divide by x to give $\dfrac{y}{x} = ax + b$ and then set $Y = \dfrac{y}{x}$ and $X = x$.

Unknown powers

This includes relations of the form $y = ax^b$ or $y = ab^x$. In these cases we have to take logs of both sides and use properties of logs to put the equation into the right form. The second example would then be:

$$\ln y \;=\; \ln(ab^x) \;=\; \ln a + \ln(b^x)$$
$$\;=\; \ln a + x\ln b$$

We would then put $Y = \ln y$ and $X = x$, giving:

$$Y = X \ln b + \ln a$$

and we would calculate a and b in the usual way.

You should now be able to answer Exercises 3, 4, 5 and 6 on p. 32.

EXERCISES

1 Find the equation of the line which:

   a   has gradient 3 and passes through (3, 4).

   b   is parallel to the line $2y = x + 5$ and passes though (2, 4).

   c   is perpendicular to the line $2y + 3x = 6$ and passes through (–1, –3).

   d   passes through the points (1, 3) and (4, 9) [find the gradient between these points and then use either of them for the known point].

2 Find the mid-point of the line joining the points $P(7, –1)$ and $Q(3, –5)$

3 Three points have coordinates $A(1, 7)$, $B(7, 5)$ and $C(0, –2)$.

   Find:

   a   the equation of the perpendicular bisector of AB

   b   the point of intersection of this perpendicular bisector and BC.

4 By drawing a suitable graph, show that the corresponding values of x and y in the table are approximately consistent with a law of the form $y = ax^b$.

x	=	12	15	22	28	35
y	=	75.9	54.3	30.6	21.3	15.3

From your graph estimate:

   a   values for a and b,

   b   the value of x when $y = 42.5$

5 Find a suitable pair of variables X and Y so that the following equations should have the form of a straight line

   a $y^2 = ax + b$ **b** $\dfrac{1}{x} + \dfrac{1}{y} = \dfrac{1}{a}$

   c $y^2 = ax^2 + bx$ **d** $xy = ax + by$

6 Choose suitable variables to transform the following equations into the forms of straight lines:

   a $y = \dfrac{x^a}{b}$ **b** $e^y = ab^x$ **c** $y = x^b e^a$

SUMMARY

We have seen how we can use a change of variable to simplify the job of evaluating constants from a set of data. Once we have done this, we can, in certain circumstances, give a mathematical model for the situation under study.

4

Trigonometry

INTRODUCTION In Module P1 you found out how to solve basic equations involving trigonometric functions. We are now going to study various identities which will allow us to change and solve a wider variety of equations. There are also applications in other fields, including integration.

Sec *x*, cosec *x* and cot *x*

There are three new trigonometric ratios with which you should be familiar. They are in fact reciprocals of the standard three ratios.

secant	shortened to	$\sec x \equiv \dfrac{1}{\cos x}$	
cosecant	shortened to	$\csc x \equiv \dfrac{1}{\sin x}$	
cotangent	shortened to	$\cot x \equiv \dfrac{1}{\tan x} \equiv \dfrac{\cos x}{\sin x}$	

To solve basic equations in these, you can substitute the appropriate identity from above:

e.g. $\sec x = \dfrac{3}{2} \;\Rightarrow\; \dfrac{1}{\cos x} = \dfrac{3}{2} \Rightarrow \cos x = \dfrac{2}{3}$

and $\cot 2x = 4 \;\Rightarrow\; \dfrac{1}{\tan 2x} = 4 \;\Rightarrow\; \tan 2x = \dfrac{1}{4}$ etc.

We will have a look at the graphs of each of these in turn, starting with $y = \sec x$.

sec x

Since $\sec x = \dfrac{1}{\cos x}$ we have some values for x for which there is no corresponding value for sec x. When $x = 90°$, for example, $\cos x = 0$ and so $\sec x = \dfrac{1}{0}$ which is not defined. We have this same situation whenever $\cos x$ is zero, i.e. at $\pm 90°$, $\pm 270°$, etc., and so the graph of $y = \sec x$ has a series of *asymptotes*, drawn in as dotted lines, to indicate that y has no value for this value of x.

Another feature of the graph is that it is *not continuous*. Just before x reaches that value of 90°, while it is still in the first quadrant, $\cos x$ is *positive* but very small. This means that $\dfrac{1}{\cos x}$ will be positive and very large.

For example, check on your calculator that $\cos 89.9° = 0.00175$

$$\Rightarrow \sec 89.9° = \dfrac{1}{\cos 89.9°} \approx 573.$$

When x is slightly larger than 90°, $\cos x$ is still small but now *negative* and consequently sec x will be large and negative: sec 90.1° for example will be –573. The minimum absolute value for sec x will correspond to the maximum absolute value of $\cos x$. So the least positive value of sec x will be $\dfrac{1}{1} = 1$, since the maximum positive value of $\cos x$ is 1; similarly the greatest negative value of sec x will be –1.

Just as $\cos x$ is even, so is sec x and it is also periodic, with the same period of 360° or 2π. Here is the graph of $y = \sec x$:

Figure 4.1

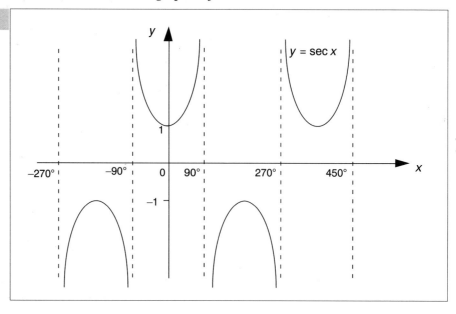

cosec x

Since the graph of $y = \sin x$ is the same as the graph of $y = \cos x$ pushed along 90°, the same applies to the graph of $y = \text{cosec } x$: here it is:

Figure 4.2

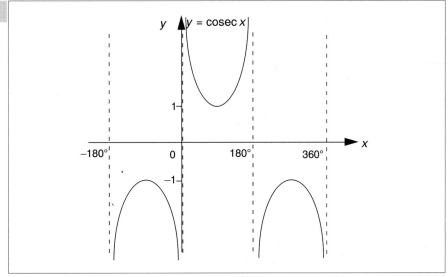

and you can see that it's the same as the graph of $y = \sec x$ pushed over 90°.

cot x

Since $\dfrac{1}{\text{something small}}$ is large and $\dfrac{1}{\text{something large}}$ is small, the graph of $\cot x$ is the precise opposite to that of $\tan x$: they meet at the points where $y = 1$ or $y = -1$.

Figure 4.3

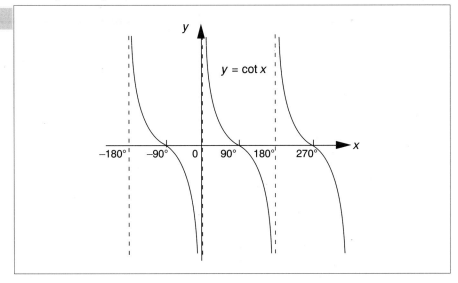

If you compare this with the graph of $y = \tan x$, you can see that where tan x was zero, cot x has an asymptote and vice versa. There is still rotational symmetry, cot x is an odd function, and it is still periodic with a period of 180° or π.

Identities between the ratios

The equations we've met so far have only contained one of the ratios – it's not going to be too long before the equations become a little more complicated and involve two or more ratios, so we need to have some means of relating them. This is not too difficult if we can remember the relationship between sides of a right-angled triangle:

Figure 4.4

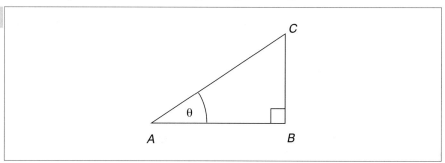

which is of course:

$$AB^2 + CB^2 = AC^2$$

When we divide everything by AC^2, this becomes:

$$\frac{AB^2}{AC^2} + \frac{CB^2}{AC^2} = \frac{AC^2}{AC^2} = 1 \qquad \dots \text{①}$$

and the two ratios on the left are familiar to us:

$$\frac{AB}{AC} = \cos \theta \quad \text{and} \quad \frac{CB}{AC} = \sin \theta$$

When we put these back into equation ① , we have:

[A]

$$\cos^2 \theta + \sin^2 \theta = 1$$

This is a very important relationship and it's certainly not the last you've seen of it. We have shown that it is true for acute angles, but in fact θ can be any angle. We can use it to work out the value for either cos θ or sin θ, if we know the other. For example, if $\cos \theta = \frac{\sqrt{5}}{3}$, we can put this value into the above equation and get:

$$\left(\frac{\sqrt{5}}{3}\right)^2 + \sin^2\theta = 1$$

$$\frac{5}{9} + \sin^2\theta = 1$$

$$\sin^2\theta = 1 - \frac{5}{9} = \frac{4}{9}$$

$$\sin\theta = \pm\frac{2}{3}$$

Note that there are two values for $\sin\theta$. When $\cos\theta$ is positive, θ is in either the first or the fourth quadrant and these alternatives give opposite signs for $\sin\theta$.

Relationship [A] is probably the most frequently used of the 'Pythagorean identities'. There are two more which you may find you use less often – it's still worth the effort of remembering them if you can. They can be derived by dividing [A] throughout by either $\cos^2\theta$ or $\sin^2\theta$.

Dividing by $\cos^2\theta$

$$\frac{\cos^2\theta}{\cos^2\theta} + \frac{\sin^2\theta}{\cos^2\theta} = \frac{1}{\cos^2\theta}$$

We can rewrite this, using the fact that:

$$\frac{\sin\theta}{\cos\theta} = \tan\theta \text{ and } \frac{1}{\cos\theta} = \sec\theta$$

[B]

$$1 + \tan^2\theta = \sec^2\theta$$

Dividing by $\sin^2\theta$

$$\frac{\cos^2\theta}{\sin^2\theta} + \frac{\sin^2\theta}{\sin^2\theta} = \frac{1}{\sin^2\theta}$$

which, putting

$$\frac{\cos\theta}{\sin\theta} = \cot\theta \text{ and } \frac{1}{\sin\theta} = \text{cosec}\,\theta$$

becomes:

[C]

$$\cot^2\theta + 1 = \text{cosec}^2\theta$$

If you can't remember all three – make sure that you know the first. You can then divide it by either $\cos^2\theta$ or $\sin^2\theta$ yourself if you need one of the others.

You should now be able to answer Exercise 1 on p. 45.

Trigonometric ratios for some common angles

A few angles crop up very frequently – it will help you very much if you can make a point of memorising the value of the various trigonometric ratios for these. If necessary, you can find them from two triangles.

Triangle 1

This has two equal sides including a right angle. If each of the sides has unit length, the remaining side, the hypotenuse, will have a length of √2. The angles other than the right-angle are each 45°.

Figure 4.5

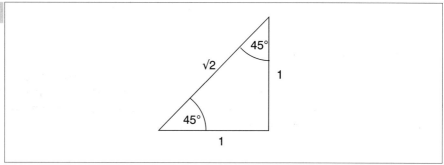

This gives:

$$\sin 45° = \frac{1}{\sqrt{2}} \qquad \cos 45° = \frac{1}{\sqrt{2}} \qquad \tan 45° = 1$$

Triangle 2

This is found by bisecting an equilateral triangle of side 2, giving a base of $\frac{1}{2} \times 2 = 1$ unit and top angle of $\frac{1}{2} \times 60° = 30°$

Figure 4.6

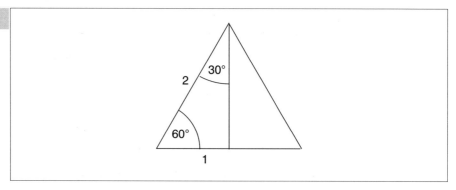

This gives:

$$\sin 30° = \frac{1}{2} \qquad \sin 60° = \frac{\sqrt{3}}{2}$$

$$\cos 30° = \frac{\sqrt{3}}{2} \qquad \cos 60° = \frac{1}{2}$$

$$\tan 30° = \frac{1}{\sqrt{3}} \qquad \tan 60° = \sqrt{3}$$

Have a look at the way that you find the value of sin 30° and the way that you find the value of cos 60° and you'll see why

$$\cos θ° = \sin (90 - θ)°$$

This means that you've less to remember – if you know that $\sin 60° = \frac{\sqrt{3}}{2}$ then you also know that cos (90 – 60)° = cos 30° has the same value.

Addition formulae

Next we look at the expansion of sine (or either of the other two main ratios) of two angles into its component parts. A particular case arises when the two angles are equal, giving a *double angle* formula, which will be very important later on (for integration, etc).

Formulae for sine

It takes a while to learn that there are certain things you just can't do to sums or differences within a function – for example, $\sqrt{a^2 + b^2} \neq a + b$ and $(a + b)^2 \neq a^2 + b^2$. In the same category comes sin $(A + B)$ – however logical a step it might seem, it's not usually sin A + sin B. There is a formula that we can use, though, and it's not too complicated:

$$\sin (A + B) \equiv \sin A \cos B + \sin B \cos A \qquad\qquad … ①$$

So for example if we wanted to find the value of sin (75°), we could put $A = 45°$ and $B = 30°$, and then:

$$\begin{aligned}
\sin (75°) &= \sin (45° + 30°) \\
&= \sin 45° \cos 30° + \sin 30° \cos 45° \\
&= \frac{1}{\sqrt{2}} \times \frac{\sqrt{3}}{2} + \frac{1}{2} \times \frac{1}{\sqrt{2}} \\
&= \frac{\sqrt{3} + 1}{2\sqrt{2}}
\end{aligned}$$

You can check this result on your calculator.

There's also a corresponding formula for sin $(A - B)$:

$$\sin (A - B) \equiv \sin A \cos B - \sin B \cos A \qquad\qquad … ②$$

To write these two identities in a single form, we put:

$$\sin (A \pm B) = \sin A \cos B \pm \sin B \cos A$$

Formulae for cosine

There are also some identities for cos $(A + B)$ and cos $(A - B)$. Notice that the signs on the right are the opposite to the signs on the left:

$$\cos (A + B) \quad = \cos A \cos B - \sin A \sin B \qquad \ldots ③$$
$$\text{and} \quad \cos (A - B) \quad = \cos A \cos B + \sin A \sin B \qquad \ldots ④$$

To show that the signs are reversed, we write the ± sign the other way up when we combine the two identities:

$$\cos (A \pm B) = \cos A \cos B \mp \sin A \sin B$$

We will now look at an example which uses these.

If $\sin A = \dfrac{4}{5}$ and $\cos B = \dfrac{12}{13}$ where angles A and B are acute, find the values of:

a sin $(A + B)$ and   **b** cos $(A - B)$

Solution   It quite often saves time, when we're given one of the trigonometric ratios, to draw the triangle containing this angle and use Pythagoras's theorem to work out the remaining side. We can then read off any of the other trigonometric ratios. In this case there are two such triangles:

Figure 4.7

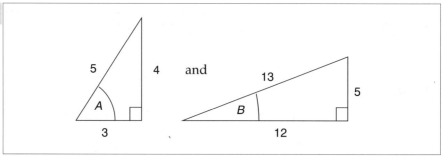

and we can see that $\cos A = \dfrac{3}{5}$ and $\sin B = \dfrac{5}{13}$.

Now we can use these to calculate the values of the ratios asked for:

a $\sin (A + B)$ $= \sin A \cos B + \cos A \sin B$

$$= \frac{4}{5} \times \frac{12}{13} + \frac{3}{5} \times \frac{5}{13} = \frac{48 + 15}{65} = \frac{63}{65}$$

b $\cos (A - B)$ $= \cos A \cos B + \sin A \sin B$

$$= \frac{3}{5} \times \frac{12}{13} + \frac{4}{5} \times \frac{5}{13} = \frac{36 + 20}{65} = \frac{56}{65}$$

Formulae for tangent

The formula for $\tan (A + B)$ is $\dfrac{\tan A + \tan B}{1 - \tan A \tan B}$

and for $\tan (A - B)$ is $\dfrac{\tan A - \tan B}{1 + \tan A \tan B}$

Noting the signs reversed on the bottom, we can combine these two as:

$$\tan A \pm B \equiv \frac{\tan A \pm \tan B}{1 \mp \tan A \tan B}$$

For example, $\tan 75° = \tan (45° + 30°)$

$$= \frac{\tan 45° + \tan 30°}{1 - \tan 45° \tan 30°} = \frac{1 + \dfrac{1}{\sqrt{3}}}{1 - \dfrac{1}{\sqrt{3}}}$$

$$= \frac{\sqrt{3} + 1}{\sqrt{3} - 1} \quad \text{on multiplying through by } \sqrt{3}$$

$$= \frac{\sqrt{3} + 1}{\sqrt{3} - 1} \times \frac{\sqrt{3} + 1}{\sqrt{3} + 1} = \frac{3 + 2\sqrt{3} + 1}{3 - 1} = \frac{4 + 2\sqrt{3}}{2} = 2 + \sqrt{3}$$

You should also be able to recognise and apply these addition formulae when they occur in equations.

Example   Find all values of θ, where $0 \leq \theta \leq \pi$, such that:

$\cos 2\theta \cos \theta = \sin 2\theta \sin \theta$

Solution   Take to one side, $\cos 2\theta \cos \theta - \sin 2\theta \sin \theta = 0$

with $A = 2\theta$, $B = \theta$, this is $\cos (A + B)$, i.e. $\cos (2\theta + \theta) = 0$ $\Rightarrow \cos 3\theta = 0$

i.e. $3\theta = \dfrac{\pi}{2}, \dfrac{3\pi}{2}, \dfrac{5\pi}{2} \Rightarrow \theta = \dfrac{\pi}{6}, \dfrac{\pi}{2}, \dfrac{5\pi}{6}$

You should now be able to answer Exercise 2 on p. 45.

Double angle formulae

One very important application of these formula is to express functions of a double angle, e.g. $\cos 2\theta$ in terms of functions of a single angle, e.g. $\cos \theta$. If we put $A = B$ into each of the three formulae for $A + B$, we'd have:

$$\sin 2A = \sin (A + A) \quad = \quad \sin A \cos A + \sin A \cos A$$
$$= \quad 2 \sin A \cos A \qquad \qquad \dots \; ⑤$$

$$\cos 2A = \cos (A + A) \quad = \quad \cos A \cos A - \sin A \sin A$$
$$= \quad \cos^2 A - \sin^2 A \qquad \dots \; ⑥$$

$$\tan 2A = \tan (A + A) \quad = \quad \frac{\tan A + \tan A}{1 - \tan A \tan A}$$
$$= \quad \frac{2 \tan A}{1 - \tan^2 A} \qquad \qquad \dots \; ⑦$$

Since $\sin^2 A + \cos^2 A = 1$, we have:

$$\cos^2 A = 1 - \sin^2 A \qquad \text{and} \qquad \sin^2 A = 1 - \cos^2 A$$

and so there are two alternative ways of writing ⑥,

$$\cos 2A = \cos^2 A - \sin^2 A = (1 - \sin^2 A) - \sin^2 A$$
$$= 1 - 2 \sin^2 A \qquad \qquad \dots \; ⑥ᵃ$$

or $\quad \cos 2A = \cos^2 A - \sin^2 A = \cos^2 A - (1 - \cos^2 A)$

$$= 2 \cos^2 A - 1 \qquad \qquad \dots \; ⑥ᵇ$$

These are important, especially the ones for $\sin 2\theta$ and $\cos 2\theta$, so try and memorise them for future use.

$$\sin 2\theta \quad \equiv \quad 2 \sin \theta \cos \theta$$

$$\cos 2\theta \quad \equiv \quad \cos^2 \theta - \sin^2 \theta$$
$$\equiv \quad 2 \cos^2 \theta - 1$$
$$\equiv \quad 1 - 2 \sin^2 \theta$$

$$\tan 2\theta \quad \equiv \quad \frac{2 \tan \theta}{1 - \tan^2 \theta}$$

We would use these, for example, to work out half-angles. Putting $\theta = 22.5°$ in the formula for $\tan 2\theta$,

$$\tan 45° = \frac{2 \tan 22.5°}{1 - \tan^2 22.5°}$$

Putting tan 22.5° $= t$ and using the fact that tan 45° $= 1$, we can rewrite this as:

$$1 = \frac{2t}{1 - t^2} \quad \text{so } 1 - t^2 = 2t \quad \Rightarrow t^2 + 2t - 1 = 0$$

Using the quadratic formula, $t = \dfrac{-2 \pm \sqrt{4 + 4}}{2} = -1 \pm \sqrt{2}$

Since tan 22.5° is positive, we take the positive value, which is $\sqrt{2} - 1$.

Other uses, and probably more important ones, occur in simplifying integrals or changing them to a more convenient form. The most usual identities to use for this are the ones involving cos 2θ, because it's much easier to integrate cos 2θ than either of cos² θ or sin² θ. We won't go further into this at the moment since we'll be dealing with it in more detail in the appropriate section. In the example below, you can see how to use half-angle formulae.

Example

Simplify $\sqrt{\dfrac{1 - \cos \theta}{1 + \cos \theta}}$

Solution

It's not immediately obvious how we're going to do this, but putting $\theta = 2A$ gives:

$$\sqrt{\frac{1 - \cos 2A}{1 + \cos 2A}} \; = \; \sqrt{\frac{2 \sin^2 A}{2 \cos^2 A}} \quad \text{from the formula}$$

$$= \; \sqrt{\tan^2 A}$$

$$= \; \tan A, \text{ provided that } \tan A \geq 0$$

$$= \; \tan \frac{\theta}{2}$$

Here's another example which uses more than one of the formulae.

Example   Express sin 3θ in terms of powers of sin θ.

Solution

$$
\begin{aligned}
\text{Sin } 3\theta \; &= \; \sin (2\theta + \theta) \\
&= \; \sin 2\theta \cos \theta + \sin \theta \cos 2\theta \\
&= \; (2 \sin \theta \cos \theta) \cos \theta + \sin \theta (1 - 2 \sin^2 \theta) \\
&= \; 2 \sin \theta \cos^2 \theta + \sin \theta (1 - 2 \sin^2 \theta) \\
&= \; 2 \sin \theta (1 - \sin^2 \theta) + \sin \theta (1 - 2 \sin^2 \theta) \\
&= \; 2 \sin \theta - 2 \sin^3 \theta + \sin \theta - 2 \sin^3 \theta \\
&= \; 3 \sin \theta - 4 \sin^3 \theta
\end{aligned}
$$

You should now be able to answer Exercises 3, 4 and 5 on p. 45.

Equations reducing to a quadratic

When we are asked to solve questions which involve mixtures of ratios, one of the standard methods which may be successful is to change the ratios in such a way as to form a quadratic equation in just one of the ratios. Let's summarise first of all the various identities between the ratios:

$$\sin^2\theta + \cos^2\theta = 1 \qquad \qquad \text{①}$$
$$1 + \tan^2\theta = \sec^2\theta \qquad \qquad \text{②}$$
$$1 + \cot^2\theta = \operatorname{cosec}^2\theta \qquad \qquad \text{③}$$
$$\cos 2\theta = 2\cos^2\theta - 1 \qquad \qquad \text{④}$$
$$= 1 - 2\sin^2\theta \qquad \qquad \text{⑤}$$

There are of course others, but these will do for the moment. Now if we have the equation:

$$4\cos 2x + 2\sin x = 3$$

we can use identity ⑤ to change this into:

$$4(1 - 2\sin^2 x) + 2\sin x = 3$$
$$4 - 8\sin^2 x + 2\sin x = 3 \qquad \qquad \text{and rearranging}$$
$$8\sin^2 x - 2\sin x - 1 = 0$$
$$(4\sin x + 1)(2\sin x - 1) = 0$$
$$\Rightarrow \qquad \sin x = -\frac{1}{4} \text{ or } \sin x = \frac{1}{2}$$

and we solve both these as normal.

If we have:

$$2\tan^2 x = 1 + \sec x$$

we can use identity ② to change this into:

$$2(\sec^2 x - 1) = 1 + \sec x$$
$$2\sec^2 x - 2 = 1 + \sec x$$
$$2\sec^2 x - \sec x - 3 = 0$$
$$(2\sec x - 3)(\sec x + 1) = 0$$
$$\sec x = \frac{3}{2} \Rightarrow \cos x = \frac{2}{3}$$

or $\qquad \sec x = -1 \Rightarrow \cos x = -1$

and again we solve these as normal, according to the limits which we're given. Note that in both cases, we formed the quadratic in the ratio that occurred as a linear term: we can change $\cos 2x$ into $\sin^2 x$ or $\tan^2 x$ into $\sec^2 x$, but we can't change just $\sin x$ or $\sec x$.

You should now be able to answer Exercises 6, 7, 8 and 9 on p. 45.

EXERCISES

1 Find the values of:

    a $\tan\theta$ when $\sec\theta = \dfrac{2}{\sqrt{3}}$ **b** $\sec\theta$ when $\tan\theta = -1$

    c $\cot\theta$ when $\operatorname{cosec}\theta = 2$ **d** $\operatorname{cosec}\theta$ when $\cot\theta = \sqrt{3}$

2 If $\sin A = \dfrac{24}{25}$ and $\cos B = \dfrac{3}{5}$ where both the angles A and B are acute, find:

    a $\cos A$ and $\tan A$ **b** $\sin B$ and $\tan B$

    c $\sin (A + B)$ **d** $\cos (A + B)$

    e $\tan (A + B)$ **f** $\tan (A - B)$

3 Given that $2 \sin (\theta - 60°) = \cos (\theta + 60°)$ show that $\tan\theta = a\sqrt{3} + b$, where a and b are integers.

4 Find the value of $\cos 2\theta$ and $\tan 2\theta$ when θ is acute and:

    a $\cos\theta = \dfrac{4}{5}$ **b** $\tan\theta = \dfrac{4}{3}$ **c** $\sin\theta = \dfrac{7}{25}$

5 Prove that:

    a $\dfrac{1 - \cos 2\theta}{\sin 2\theta} = \tan\theta$ **b** $\cos 3\theta = 4 \cos^3 \theta - 3 \cos\theta$

    c $\dfrac{2 \tan\theta}{1 + \tan^2\theta} = \sin 2\theta$ **d** $\dfrac{1 + \cos\theta}{\sin\theta} = \cot\dfrac{\theta}{2}$

6 Find all the angles in the range $0°$ to $360°$ inclusive which satisfy:

    $4 \cos 2x + 2 \sin x = 3$

7 Find all the solutions in the interval $0° \le \theta \le 360°$ of the equation:

    $2 \sin^2\theta + 5 \cos\theta + 1 = 0$ (Hint: put $\sin^2 y = 1.75$)

8 Find values of θ in range $-\pi < \theta < \pi$ for which $\sec^2\theta = 3 \tan\theta - 1$

9 Find values of θ in range $-180° < \theta < 180°$ for which $\cot^2\theta + \operatorname{cosec}\theta = 5$.

SUMMARY

We have now extended the range of trigonometric equations we can solve: the relationships between the various identities are particularly important as they crop up again and again in the work to come.

5

Differentiation

We are going to extend our list of functions for which we can find the gradient to include the trigonometric functions. We shall also see how we can differentiate various combinations of our standard functions and apply these techniques for some more advanced results

Standard functions

We have seen how we can derive the derivative of powers of x by seeing that the gradient of certain chords tends to a definite limit.

In a similar way, we can find the gradient function for each of the other functions that we've met. Let's put the ones we already know together with these new ones and make a table for reference.

$$\text{If } y = x^n \qquad \text{then } \frac{dy}{dx} = nx^{n-1}$$

$$y = e^x \qquad \text{then } \frac{dy}{dx} = e^x$$

$$y = \ln x \qquad \text{then } \frac{dy}{dx} = \frac{1}{x}$$

$$y = \sin x \qquad \text{then } \frac{dy}{dx} = \cos x$$

$$y = \cos x \qquad \text{then } \frac{dy}{dx} = -\sin x$$

$$y = \tan x \qquad \text{then } \frac{dy}{dx} = \sec^2 x$$

For the last three trig functions, x must be n radians.

Example Find the gradients of the curves given by:

a $\quad y = 5x^2 - 3 \qquad$ at $\quad x = 2$

b $\quad y = \ln x \qquad$ at $\quad x = 3$

c $\quad y = \cos x \qquad$ at $\quad x = \dfrac{\pi}{4}$

Solution

a If $y = 5x^2 - 3$,   then $\dfrac{dy}{dx} = 10x = 20$ when $x = 2$

b If $y = \ln x$,   then $\dfrac{dy}{dx} = \dfrac{1}{x} = \dfrac{1}{3}$ when $x = 3$

c If $y = \cos x$,   then $\dfrac{dy}{dx} = -\sin x = -\dfrac{1}{\sqrt{2}}$ when $x = \dfrac{\pi}{4}$

You should now be able to answer Exercise 1 on p. 57.

You will be using these results over and over again and will find it useful to learn them. We'll see now how we can find the derivative of various combinations, starting with products.

Differentiation of a product

If y is the product of two functions of x, u and v say, so that $y = uv$, then

$$\frac{dy}{dx} = u\frac{dv}{dx} + v\frac{du}{dx}$$

So that if $y = x^2 \sin x$,

$$\frac{dy}{dx} = x^2 \cos x + 2x \sin x$$

and if $y = \ln x \tan x$, then

$$\frac{dy}{dx} = \ln x \sec^2 x + \frac{1}{x}\tan x$$

Note that since the two terms are added, it doesn't matter which part you differentiate and which keeps constant first of all.

You should now be able to answer Exercise 2 on page 57.

Differentiation of a quotient

There is a corresponding formula for quotients:

If u and v are functions of x and $y = \dfrac{u}{v}$

then $\dfrac{dy}{dx} = \dfrac{v\dfrac{du}{dx} - u\dfrac{dv}{dx}}{v^2}$

So if $y = \dfrac{\sin x}{x^2}$, $\dfrac{dy}{dx} = \dfrac{x^2 \cos x - \sin x \cdot 2x}{x^4}$

$$= \dfrac{x \cos x - 2 \sin x}{x^3}$$

Note that the negative sign between the terms on top of the fraction means that order is important here. It also means that you have to be a little careful with signs sometimes, giving each term its own bracket. Let's look at an example of this.

Example   Find $\dfrac{dy}{dx}$ when $y = \dfrac{1 - x^2}{x^2}$

Solution $\dfrac{dy}{dx} = \dfrac{x^2 (-2x) - (1 - x^2) \, 2x}{x^4}$

$$= \dfrac{-2x^3 - 2x + 2x^3}{x^4} = \dfrac{-2x}{x^4} = \dfrac{-2}{x^3}$$

It's very easy if you don't put the terms in brackets to miss one of the minus signs.

You should now be able to answer Exercise 3 on page 57.

Implicit differentiation

The functions we've differentiated so far have given one of the variables, usually y, explicitly in terms of the other variable, usually x, in the form of $y = f(x)$. When y is mixed in with the x's, given implicitly, we have to expand our technique of differentiation so that we can still find the gradient function at any point.

When we talk about differentiating some function, x^3, we assume that the differentiation is with respect to the same variable, x, and write:

$$\dfrac{d(x^3)}{dx} = 3x^2$$

If we want to differentiate the same function with respect to another variable, t say, we differentiate as before with respect to x, but then multiply by x differentiated with respect to t:

$$\dfrac{d(x^3)}{dt} = \dfrac{d(x^3)}{dx} \times \dfrac{dx}{dt} = 3x^2 \dfrac{dx}{dt}$$

You can see that it looks as though the dx's 'cancel' on the right-hand side to give the left-hand side. Let's take another example and differentiate ln u with respect to v:

$$\frac{d(\ln u)}{dv} = \frac{d(\ln u)}{du} \times \frac{du}{dv} = \frac{1}{u}\frac{du}{dv}$$

We'll use this to find $\frac{dy}{dx}$ from an expression where the x's and y's are mixed together, such as:

$$x^3 + 3y^2 - 2x - 5y = 3$$

If we differentiate term by term with respect to x, which we should now be able to do without too much trouble, we get the following:

$$3x^2 + 6y\frac{dy}{dx} - 2 - 5\frac{dy}{dx} = 0$$

Rearranging gives: $6y\dfrac{dy}{dx} - 5\dfrac{dy}{dx} = 2 - 3x^2$

Factorising gives: $(6y - 5)\dfrac{dy}{dx} = 2 - 3x^2$

Dividing gives: $\dfrac{dy}{dx} = \dfrac{2 - 3x^2}{6y - 5}$

This is quite straightforward provided we remember:

a   to put $\dfrac{dy}{dx}$ after differentiating a y term, and

b   that constants differentiated are zero.

But when there are mixtures of x's and y's in the same term, for example $3x^3y^2$ it is necessary to differentiate using the product rule

$$\frac{d(3x^3y^2)}{dx} = \underset{\text{constant}}{3x^3} \times \underset{\text{differentiated}}{y^2} + \underset{\text{differentiated}}{3x^3} \times \underset{\text{constant}}{y^2}$$

$$= \quad 3x^3 \times 2y\frac{dy}{dx} + 9x^2y^2$$

$$= \quad 6x^3y\frac{dy}{dx} + 9x^2y^2$$

You should now be able to answer Exercise 4 on page 57.

A function of a function

When we looked at implicit differentiation we found that we could differentiate a function of one variable with respect to another variable, for example:

$$\frac{d(u^3)}{dx} = 3u^2\frac{du}{dx}$$

This is going to be useful now, because we can use this to differentiate something like:

$$y = (1 + x^2)^3$$

which at the moment we can't do directly. If we change the variable, however, we can temporarily simplify this expression. Put in $u = 1 + x^2$, so that now $y = u^3$.

Differentiating both sides with respect to x gives:

$$\frac{dy}{dx} = 3u^2 \frac{du}{dx}$$

as we saw above. But $\frac{du}{dx} = 2x$, so we can write this:

$$\frac{dy}{dx} = 3u^2 \times 2x$$
$$= 3(1 + x^2)^2 \times 2x$$
$$= 6x (1 + x^2)^2$$

which is once again in terms of x as we wanted. We will now try some more in the following example.

Example

Differentiate:

a $\ln (1 + 2x^3)$ **b** $\sin (x^2 - 1)$

Solution

a   Put $y = \ln (1 + 2x^3)$ and $u = 1 + 2x^3$ so that:

$$y = \ln u$$

Differentiating with respect to x,

$$\frac{dy}{dx} = \frac{1}{u} \times \frac{du}{dx}$$

But $u = 1 + 2x^3$, so $\frac{du}{dx} = 6x^2$ and $\frac{dy}{dx} = \frac{1}{u} \times 6x^2$

$$= \frac{6x^2}{1 + 2x^3}$$

b   Putting $y = \sin (x^2 - 1)$ and $u = x^2 - 1$, we have:

$$y = \sin u, \text{ so that}$$
$$\frac{dy}{dx} = \cos u \times \frac{du}{dx}$$
$$\frac{du}{dx} = 2x \quad \text{and} \quad \frac{dy}{dx} = \cos u \times 2x$$
$$= 2x \cos (x^2 - 1)$$

Most of the differentiation we meet with will involve expressions of this type and we need to be able to deal with them quickly and accurately. We will now look at some of these to help you understand them:

a   If $y = e^{5x}$;   put $u = 5x$ so that $y = e^u$

then $\dfrac{dy}{dx}$ $= e^u \times \dfrac{du}{dx}$: $u = 5x \Rightarrow \dfrac{du}{dx} = 5$

$= e^u \times 5$

$= 5e^{5x}$

b   If $y = e^{\sin x}$;   put $u = \sin x$ so that $y = e^u$

then $\dfrac{dy}{dx}$ $= e^u \times \dfrac{du}{dx}$: $u = \sin x \Rightarrow \dfrac{du}{dx} = \cos x$

$= e^u \times \cos x$

$= \cos x \, e^{\sin x}$

Using $\rightarrow$ to mean differentiation with respect to x, we could write these two as:

$e^{5x} \rightarrow 5e^{5x}$

$e^{\sin x} \rightarrow \cos x e^{\sin x}$

In general we could write this as

$e^{\text{function}} \rightarrow$ function differentiated $\times \, e^{\text{function}}$

or $e^{f(x)} \rightarrow f'(x) \, e^{f(x)}$

where $f(x)$ represents a function and $f'(x)$ represents the function differentiated.

Using this as a model, we can write some of the simpler examples of this type straight down, for example:

$e^{3x^2} \quad \rightarrow \quad 6xe^{3x^2}$

$e^{1-x} \quad \rightarrow \quad -e^{1-x}$

$e^{\tan x} \quad \rightarrow \quad \sec^2 x \, e^{\tan x}$

Using the same shorthand, we can draw up another table for the standard functions.

$$[f(x)]^n \rightarrow f'(x) \times n[f(x)]^{n-1}$$

$$e^{f(x)} \rightarrow f'(x) \times e^{f(x)}$$

$$\ln f(x) \rightarrow f'(x) \times \frac{1}{f(x)}$$

$$\sin f(x) \rightarrow f'(x) \times \cos f(x)$$

$$\cos f(x) \rightarrow f'(x) \times -\sin f(x)$$

$$\tan f(x) \rightarrow f'(x) \times \sec^2 f(x)$$

Taking a particular example of each to show them in action:

$$(1 + 3x^2)^5 \rightarrow 6x \times 5(1 + 3x^2)^4 = 30x\,(1 + 3x^2)^4$$

$$e^{1+3x^2} \rightarrow 6xe^{1+3x^2}$$

$$\ln(1 + 3x^2) \rightarrow \frac{6x}{1 + 3x^2}$$

$$\sin(1 + 3x^2) \rightarrow 6x \cos(1 + 3x^2)$$

$$\cos(1 + 3x^2) \rightarrow -6x \sin(1 + 3x^2)$$

$$\tan(1 + 3x^2) \rightarrow 6x \sec^2(1 + 3x^2)$$

You should now be able to answer Exercises 5, 6 and 7 on p. 57.

Partial fractions and differentiation

In order to differentiate a function like:

$$y = \frac{5x - 7}{(x - 2)(x - 1)}$$

and especially if you want to find the higher order derivatives like $\frac{d^2y}{dx^2}, \frac{d^3y}{dx^3}$ etc, it is often easier to express the function in partial fractions first of all and then differentiate these parts separately. For the above function, for example:

$$y = \frac{5x - 7}{(x - 2)(x - 1)} \equiv \frac{A}{x - 2} + \frac{B}{x - 1} \equiv \frac{A(x - 1) + B(x - 2)}{(x - 2)(x - 1)}$$

i.e. $5x - 7 \equiv A(x - 1) + B(x - 2)$

Putting $x = 1$: $-2 = -B \Rightarrow B = 2$

 $x = 2$: $3 = A \Rightarrow A = 3$

i.e. $y = \dfrac{3}{x - 2} + \dfrac{2}{x - 1}$

By expressing these fractions as powers of brackets, we can differentiate as many times as we like quite easily:

$$y = 3(x - 2)^{-1} + 2(x - 1)^{-1}$$

$$\frac{dy}{dx} = -3(x - 2)^{-2} - 2(x - 1)^{-2}$$

$$\frac{d^2y}{dx^2} = 6(x - 2)^{-3} + 4(x - 1)^{-3}$$

$$\frac{d^3y}{dx^3} = -18(x - 2)^{-4} - 12(x - 1)^{-4} \qquad \text{etc.}$$

You should now be able to answer Exercise 8 on p. 57.

Tangents and normals

A line which just touches a curve at a given point is called a *tangent*.

Figure 5.1

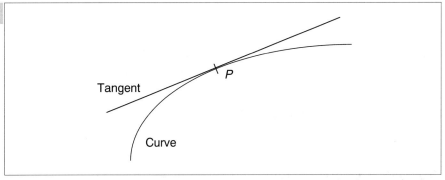

Since the gradients of the tangent and of the curve at this point are the same, we can quite easily find this common gradient by differentiating the equation of the curve. Then knowing the gradient of the tangent and a point through which it passes, we can find the equation of the tangent.

Example   Find the equation of the tangent to the curve given by:

$$y = x^3 - x \quad \text{at the point where } x = 2$$

Solution   When $x = 2$, $y = 2^3 - 2 = 6$, so the tangent passes through the point (2,6).

The gradient of the curve is given by:

$$\frac{dy}{dx} = 3x^2 - 1$$

and so when $x = 2$, the gradient will be 11. This is, by definition, the gradient of the tangent at this point.

So we have to find an equation of a line whose gradient is 11 passing through the point (2,6).

Using the formula:

$$\text{Gradient} = \frac{y - y\text{-}coordinate}{x - x\text{-}coordinate}$$

we have

$$11 = \frac{y - 6}{x - 2}$$

i.e.

$$y - 6 = 11(x - 2)$$
$$= 11x - 22$$

Then $y = 11x - 16$ is the equation of the tangent.

Here's a sketch to illustrate the curve and this tangent (not to scale).

Figure 5.2

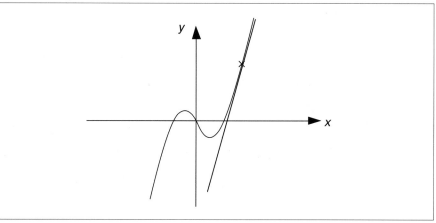

The *normal* to a curve at a given point is the line perpendicular to the tangent at this point.

Figure 5.3

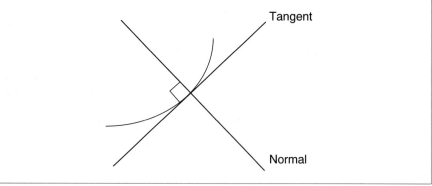

We can find the gradient of the normal by using the fact that if two lines are perpendicular, the product of their gradient is –1:

$$\text{Grad}_{\text{TANGENT}} \times \text{Grad}_{\text{NORMAL}} = -1$$

i.e.

$$\text{Grad}_{\text{NORMAL}} = \frac{-1}{\text{Grad}_{\text{TANGENT}}}$$

So in the last case, since the gradient of the tangent was 11, the gradient of the normal would be $\dfrac{-1}{11}$ and the equation of the normal would be

$$\frac{-1}{11} = \frac{y-6}{x-2}$$

i.e. $\quad -1(x-2) = 11(y-6)$

$\qquad\qquad -x + 2 = 11y - 66$

or $\qquad y = \dfrac{68 - x}{11}$

We will work through another example and then you should be able to try some.

Example	Find the equation of the normal to the curve given by $y = \dfrac{x-1}{2x+1}$ at the point where $x = 4$.

Solution	$\dfrac{dy}{dx} = \dfrac{(2x+1)\,1 - (x-1)\,2}{(2x+1)^2} = \dfrac{3}{(2x+1)^2} = \dfrac{1}{27}$ when $x = 4$

This is the gradient of the *tangent*; the gradient of the normal will be -27 when $x = 4$, $y = \dfrac{3}{9} = \dfrac{1}{3}$ and the equation of the normal is

$$y - \frac{1}{3} = -27\,(x-4) \Rightarrow 3y - 1 = -81(x-4)$$

i.e. $\quad 3y + 81x = 325$

You should now be able to answer Exercises 9 and 10 on p. 58.

Functions given implicitly

Provided we have the coordinates of the point – or at least one of the coordinates so that we can work out the other – we can find a numerical value for the gradient from the equation involving $\dfrac{dy}{dx}$. We can then find the tangent and normal in the same way as before. We will now look at an example of this.

Example	Find the equation of the normal at the point $(1,1)$ to the curve given by:

$$9x^2y + 6xy^2 = 15$$

Solution	We differentiate with respect to x, giving:

$$18xy + 9x^2\frac{dy}{dx} + 6y^2 + 12xy\frac{dy}{dx} = 0$$

We could rearrange this to give an expression for $\frac{dy}{dx}$, but actually it's probably quicker to substitute the values for x and y straight in:

$$18 + 9\frac{dy}{dx} + 6 + 12\frac{dy}{dx} = 0$$

$$24 + 21\frac{dy}{dx} = 0$$

$$\frac{dy}{dx} = -\frac{24}{21} = -\frac{8}{7}$$

This is the gradient of the curve at the point $(1,1)$, that is, the gradient of the tangent. We want the gradient of the normal. Since:

$$\text{Grad}_{\text{TANGENT}} \times \text{Grad}_{\text{NORMAL}} = -1$$

$$\frac{-8}{7}\text{Grad}_{\text{NORMAL}} = -1 \quad \Rightarrow G_{\text{NORMAL}} = \frac{7}{8}$$

The equation of the normal is then:

$$(y - 1) = \frac{7}{8}(x - 1) \Rightarrow 8y - 8 = 7x - 7 \Rightarrow 8y = 7x + 1$$

Further derivatives

To complete the list of standard functions that you should know how to differentiate, let's look first of all at the group of functions that have the form $y = a^x$. Given that a is constant, we can write this as:

$$y = e^{\ln(a^x)} \quad \text{(since e and ln are inverses of each other, } e^{\ln x} = x\text{)}$$
$$= e^{x\ln a} \quad \text{by the properties of lns.}$$

Since $\ln a$ is constant, we can differentiate this directly.

$$\frac{dy}{dx} = \ln a\, e^{x\ln a} = a^x \ln a$$

Note that if $a = e$, this reduces to e^x since $\ln e = 1$ (which is what we would expect).

For example, if $y = 3^x$ then $\frac{dy}{dx} = 3^x \ln 3$.

EXERCISES

1 Find the gradient of the curve given by:

   a $y = 2x^3 - 6x$ when $x = 2$

   b $y = e^x$ when $x = 1.5$ (to two decimal places)

   c $y = \sin x$ when $x = \dfrac{\pi}{3}$

   d $y = \tan x$ when $x = \dfrac{\pi}{6}$

2 Find $\dfrac{dy}{dx}$ when $y =$

   a $x^3 \cos x$ **b** $e^x \sin x$ **c** $x^3 e^x$ **d** $x \ln x$

3 Find $\dfrac{dy}{dx}$ when $y =$

   a $\dfrac{x}{x+1}$ **b** $\dfrac{x^2}{1-x^2}$ **c** $\dfrac{1-x}{1+x}$ **d** $\dfrac{e^x}{x^3}$ **e** $\dfrac{\ln x}{x}$

4 Find an expression for $\dfrac{dy}{dx}$ in terms of x and y for:

   a $3x^2 - 6xy + 2y^2 = 5$

   b $e^x y - e^y x = 1$

   c $\dfrac{1}{x} + \dfrac{1}{y} = e^y$

5 Differentiate with respect to x by changing the variable:

   a $(1 + 3x)^4$ **b** e^{x^2} **c** $\tan(x^2 - 1)$ **d** $\cos(e^x)$

6 Write down the derivatives of the following functions:

   a e^{3x} **b** e^{-x} **c** $e^{\cos x}$ **d** e^{x-x^3} **e** $e^{\ln x}$ **f** 5^x

7 Write down the derivatives of:

   a $(1 - x^4)^3$ **b** $\sqrt{4 - x^2}$ **c** $(1 + \sin x)^4$ **d** e^{4+x^2} **e** $e^{1-\cos x}$

   f $\ln(1 + 5x)$ **g** $\ln(4 - x^2)$ **h** $\sin(1 - 4x^2)$ **i** $\sin(3 + 2e^x)$

   j $\cos(x^3)$ **k** $\cos\left(\dfrac{\pi}{4} - x\right)$ **l** $\tan(3x + 2)$ **m** $\tan(3 - \ln x)$

8 Express $y = \dfrac{2x + 10}{(x-3)(x+1)}$ in partial fractions and hence find the

   value of $\dfrac{d^3y}{dx^3}$ when $x = 2$

9 a Find the equations of the tangent and normal to the curve
$y = x^3 + x + 1$ at the point where $x = 1$

b Find the equations of the tangent and normal to the curve
$y = x + \sin x$ at the point where $x = \dfrac{\pi}{4}$

10 Find the equations of the tangent and normal to the curve given by:
$3x^2y^3 - x^3y^2 = 4x$ at the point (2,1).

SUMMARY

We know now how to find the differential of the majority of the functions we shall meet with in our studies: it is particularly important that you learn how to differentiate composite functions, including powers of functions, quickly and accurately.

Integration

INTRODUCTION   We are going to continue the work started in the previous module: we will learn how to integrate other standard functions and the various techniques that have evolved for finding the integral of more complicated expressions. Two of the applications of integration will then be covered: finding the areas underneath curves and the volumes when these curves are rotated around the axes.

Standard functions

We can find many of the standard integrals by remembering the derivative and reversing, so that:

$$\frac{d(\ln x)}{dx} = \frac{1}{x} \qquad \Rightarrow \qquad \int \frac{1}{x}\, dx \qquad = \ln x + C, x > 0$$

$$\frac{d(e^x)}{dx} = e^x \qquad \Rightarrow \qquad \int e^x\, dx \qquad = e^x + C$$

$$\frac{d(\sin x)}{dx} = \cos x \qquad \Rightarrow \qquad \int \cos x\, dx \quad = \sin x + C$$

$$\frac{d(\cos x)}{dx} = -\sin x \qquad \Rightarrow \qquad \int \sin x\, dx \quad = -\cos x + C$$

$$\frac{d(\tan x)}{dx} = \sec^2 x \qquad \Rightarrow \qquad \int \sec^2 x\, dx \quad = \tan x + C$$

Using this same method, we can work out a few slightly more complicated examples as well:

$$\frac{d(\ln (x + 4))}{dx} = \frac{1}{x + 4} \qquad \Rightarrow \int \frac{1}{x + 4}\, dx \quad = \ln (x + 4) + C$$

$$\frac{d(e^{3x})}{dx} = 3e^{3x} \qquad \Rightarrow \int e^{3x}\, dx \quad = \frac{1}{3} e^{3x} + C$$

$$\frac{d(\sin 2x)}{dx} = 2 \cos 2x \qquad \Rightarrow \int \cos 2x\, dx = \frac{1}{2} \sin 2x + C$$

$$\frac{d(\cos 5x)}{dx} = -5 \sin 5x \qquad \Rightarrow \int \sin 5x\, dx \quad = -\frac{1}{5} \cos 5x + C$$

$$\frac{d(\tan 7x)}{dx} = 7 \sec^2 7x \qquad \Rightarrow \int \sec^2 7x\, dx \quad = \frac{1}{7} \tan 7x + C$$

One integral which crops up quite frequently is of the form:

$$\int (ax + b)^n dx, \quad n \neq -1$$

We can find this by thinking of differentiating a similar term:

If $\quad y = (ax + b)^m \quad$ then $\dfrac{dy}{dx} = m(ax + b)^{m-1} \times a$

$$= ma\,(ax + b)^{m-1}$$

In other words, we reduce the power by one and have the product of the old power and the x-coefficient in front. To integrate, we have to reverse this:

$$\int (ax + b)^n\, dx \quad = \quad \frac{(ax + b)^{n+1}}{a(n + 1)} + C$$

so that, for example, $\quad \displaystyle\int (2x - 5)^9\, dx \quad = \quad \dfrac{(2x - 5)^{10}}{2 \times 10} + C$

$$= \quad \frac{1}{20}\,(2x - 5)^{10} + C$$

and $\quad \displaystyle\int \frac{1}{\sqrt{1 - 4x}}\, dx \quad = \quad \int (1 - 4x)^{-\frac{1}{2}}\, dx$

$$= \quad \frac{(1 - 4x)^{-\frac{1}{2}}}{(-4)\left(\frac{1}{2}\right)} + C$$

$$= \quad \frac{-1}{2}\,(1 - 4x)^{-\frac{1}{2}} + C$$

An extremely important exception to this is when $n = -1$: we have to remember that this comes from differentiating a ln, so that for example

if $\quad y = \ln (3x - 2) \quad$ then $\dfrac{dy}{dx} \quad = \quad \dfrac{3}{3x - 2}$

$$\Rightarrow \int \frac{3}{3x - 2}\, dx \quad = \quad \ln (3x - 2) + C \quad \text{for } 3x - 2 > 0$$

or $\quad \displaystyle\int \frac{1}{3x - 2}\, dx \quad = \quad \frac{1}{3}\ln (3x - 2) + C$

We'll make a table of these standard functions, shown at the top of the next page. It is of course best to remember these: you will be using them over and over again. We're going to have a look at a method by which we can integrate certain products.

$$\int e^{ax}\, dx = \frac{1}{a} e^{ax} + C$$

$$\int \sin ax\, dx = \frac{-1}{a} \cos ax + C$$

$$\int \cos ax\, dx = \frac{1}{a} \sin ax + C$$

$$\int (ax + b)^n\, dx = \frac{(ax + b)^{n+1}}{a(n + 1)} \quad \text{if } n \neq -1$$

$$\int \frac{1}{ax + b}\, dx = \frac{1}{a} \ln | ax + b | + C$$

(In the last case the modulus sign ensures that we don't have a ln of a negative number.)

You should now be able to answer Exercise 1 on p. 78.

Integration by parts

The formula for this comes from integrating the rule for differentiating products. It can be written:

$$\int u \frac{dv}{dx}\, dx = uv - \int v \frac{du}{dx}\, dx$$

Basically, it means that we take one of the terms and differentiate $\left[u \rightarrow \dfrac{du}{dx} \right]$

and the other of the terms making up the product and integrate $\left[\dfrac{dv}{dx} \rightarrow v \right]$.

The new product, if we have chosen u and $\dfrac{dv}{dx}$ wisely, can turn out to be easier to integrate. Let's have a look at an example of this:

Example Evaluate $\displaystyle\int x \cos 2x\, dx$.

Solution Put $\quad u = x$ and $\dfrac{dv}{dx} = \cos 2x$

$\therefore \dfrac{du}{dx} = 1$ and $v = \dfrac{1}{2} \sin 2x \quad$ (forget $+ C$)

61

Now substitute in the 'by parts' formula to get:

$$\int x \cos 2x \, dx \;=\; \frac{x}{2}\sin 2x - \int \frac{1}{2}\sin 2x \, dx$$

$$=\; \frac{x}{2}\sin 2x - \frac{1}{2}\int \sin 2x \, dx \quad \text{(Take constants outside}$$

the integral if possible)

$$\therefore \quad \int x \cos 2x \, dx \;=\; \frac{x}{2}\sin 2x + \frac{1}{4}\cos 2x + C$$

Example Find $\int xe^{-2x}\, dx$

Solution

Put $u = x$ and $\dfrac{dv}{dx} = e^{-2x}$

$$\therefore \quad \frac{du}{dx} = 1 \text{ and } v = -\frac{1}{2}e^{-2x} \quad \text{(forget + C)}$$

Now substitute in the 'by parts' formula to get:

$$\int xe^{-2x}\, dx \;=\; -\frac{x}{2}e^{-2x} - \int -\frac{1}{2}e^{-2x}\, dx$$

$$=\; -\frac{x}{2}e^{-2x} + \frac{1}{2}\int e^{-2x}\, dx. \text{ (Always simplify)}$$

$$\therefore \quad \int xe^{-2x}\, dx \;=\; -\frac{x}{2}e^{-2x} - \frac{1}{4}e^{-2x} + C.$$

Note that in both these examples we have taken u to be x : this is mostly true, except in the case where one of the terms of the product is $\ln x$. In this case, we take u to be $\ln x$ and integrate the power of x:

Example Find $\int x^5 \ln x \, dx$

Solution

$u = \ln x$ and $\dfrac{dv}{dx} = x^5$

then $\dfrac{du}{dx} = \dfrac{1}{x}$ and $v = \dfrac{x^6}{6}$

i.e. $\displaystyle\int x^5 \ln x \, dx \;=\; \frac{x^6}{6}\ln x - \int \frac{1}{x} \times \frac{x^6}{6}\, dx$

$$=\; \frac{x^6}{6}\ln x - \frac{1}{6}\int x^5 \, dx$$

$$=\; \frac{x^6}{6}\ln x - \frac{1}{36}x^6 + C$$

$$=\; \frac{x^6}{36}\,(6\ln x - 1) + C$$

Integration by parts – twice

When the x term turns out to be x^2, we can sometimes find the integral by integrating twice by parts, for example:

$$\int x^2 e^{2x} dx \qquad u = x^2 \qquad \frac{dv}{dx} = e^{2x}$$

$$= \frac{1}{2} x^2 e^{2x} - \int 2x \times \frac{1}{2} e^{2x} dx \qquad \frac{du}{dx} = 2x \qquad v = \frac{1}{2} e^{2x}$$

$$= \frac{1}{2} x^2 e^{2x} - \int x e^{2x} dx \leftarrow \text{We now find this integral using the by}$$

parts method

$$u = x \qquad \frac{dv}{dx} = e^{2x}$$

$$\frac{du}{dx} = 1 \qquad v = \frac{1}{2} e^{2x}$$

and our original integral becomes:

$$\frac{1}{2} x^2 e^{2x} - \left(\frac{1}{2} x e^{2x} - \frac{1}{2} \int e^{2x} \right)$$

$$= \frac{1}{2} x^2 e^{2x} - \frac{1}{2} x e^{2x} + \frac{1}{4} e^{2x} + C$$

$$= \frac{e^{2x}}{4} \left(2x^2 - 2x + 1 \right) + C$$

There is one other 'trick' that you have to know. Sometimes a single function occurs and you still integrate as a product; the second term of the product is taken as 1:

e.g. $\int \ln x \, dx \qquad u = \ln x \qquad \frac{dv}{dx} = 1$

$$= \int (\ln x \times 1) \, dx \qquad \frac{du}{dx} = \frac{1}{x} \qquad v = x$$

$$= x \ln x - \int \frac{1}{x} \times x \, dx$$

$$= x \ln x - x + C$$

You should now be able to answer Exercises 2, 3, 4 and 5 on p. 78.

Use of partial fractions

Integrals with partial fractions

Use of partial fractions with integration is one of the standard exam questions – you must learn to recognise this type of integral. All the following examples:

$$\int \frac{ax\ dx}{(x-1)\ (x+2)} \quad \text{or} \quad \int \frac{1}{x^2-5x+6}\ dx \quad \text{or} \quad \int \frac{x-1}{x^2-9}\ dx$$

$$\text{or} \quad \int \frac{1}{1-x^2}\ dx \quad \text{or} \quad \int \frac{x^2}{(4-x)\ (x+3)}\ dx \quad \text{or} \int \frac{x^3+1}{x^2-1}\ dx$$

where the bottom of the fraction consists of two linear factors, or would do after factorising, are integrals of this kind. Let's have a look at a basic example.

Example

Show that: $\displaystyle\int_1^2 \frac{6x+7}{(2x-1)\ (x+2)}\ dx = \ln 12$

Solution

We have a look first of all at the highest powers occurring on the top and bottom of the fraction – that on the top is less than that on the bottom in this case, so we don't need a preliminary division.

$$\text{Suppose} \quad \frac{6x+7}{(2x-1)\ (x+2)} \quad \equiv \quad \frac{A}{2x-1} + \frac{B}{x+2}$$

$$\equiv \quad \frac{A(x+2)+B(2x-1)}{(2x-1)\ (x+2)}$$

i.e. $\quad 6x+7 \quad \equiv \quad A(x+2)+B(2x-1)$

$x = -2: \qquad -5 = -5B \qquad \Rightarrow \qquad B = 1$

$x = \dfrac{1}{2}: \qquad 10 = \dfrac{5A}{2} \qquad \Rightarrow \qquad A = 4$

Then $\displaystyle\int_1^2 \frac{6x+7}{(2x-1)\ (x+2)}\ dx \quad = \quad \int_1^2 \left(\frac{4}{(2x-1)} + \frac{1}{x+2}\right) dx$

$$= \quad \left[2\ \ln(2x-1) + \ln\ (x+2)\right]_1^2$$

$$= \quad (2\ \ln 3 + \ln 4) - (2\ \ln 1 + \ln 3)$$

$$= \quad \ln 3 + \ln 4$$

$$= \quad \ln 12$$

You should now be able to answer Exercises 6, 7 and 8 on p. 78.

Recognition

We know that if $y = \ln f(x)$, then $\dfrac{dy}{dx} = \dfrac{f'(x)}{f(x)}$, e.g. if $y = \ln (1 + x^2)$

then $\dfrac{dy}{dx} = \dfrac{2x}{1+x^2}$.

If we reverse this procedure, we have:

$$\int \frac{f'(x)}{f(x)} \, dx = \ln | f(x) | + C, \text{ for example } \int \frac{2x}{1 + x^2} \, dx = \ln (1 + x^2) + C$$

We may need to adjust the constant: $\int \frac{x^2}{1 + x^3} \, dx = \frac{1}{3} \ln | 1 + x^3 | + C$

and we may need to rewrite the integral first of all to put it into this form, e.g.

$$\int \cot x \, dx = \int \frac{\cos x}{\sin x} \, dx = \ln | \sin x | + C$$

Substitution

It's not often in exams that we're presented with an integral that can be done straight away, with no preparatory work: usually they require a changing round of some description. The method of substitution that we study here is one that will enable us to solve quite a few types of otherwise difficult integrals.

Changing the variable

We can sometimes transform an integral containing an awkward function into something which is easier to handle by changing the variable. Let's compare, for example, the two integrals:

$$\int \frac{x}{\sqrt{x-1}} \, dx \quad \text{and} \quad \int \frac{x+1}{\sqrt{x}} \, dx$$

We can integrate the one on the right by separating and dividing:

$$\int \frac{x+1}{\sqrt{x}} \, dx \quad = \quad \int \left(\frac{x}{\sqrt{x}} + \frac{1}{\sqrt{x}} \right) dx$$

$$= \quad \int \left(\sqrt{x} + \frac{1}{\sqrt{x}} \right) dx$$

$$= \quad \int \left(x^{\frac{1}{2}} + x^{-\frac{1}{2}} \right) dx$$

$$= \quad \frac{2}{3} x^{\frac{3}{2}} + 2x^{\frac{1}{2}} + C$$

The one on the left is not obvious – we can't use the same method because the function inside the square root is too complicated. So we change this by putting $u = x - 1$: then we have to think about the rest of the integral. The x-term on the top is OK because if $u = x - 1$, $x = u + 1$ and now our original integral:

$$\int \frac{x}{\sqrt{x-1}} \, dx \quad \text{has become} \quad \int \left(\frac{u+1}{\sqrt{u}} \right) dx$$

We can't integrate this as it stands, because the dx outside the bracket means that the integration is supposed to be with respect to the old variable, x, and we want to integrate with respect to u. Since:

$$dx = \frac{dx}{du} \times du$$

we can write $\dfrac{dx}{du}\, du$ instead of dx. We have to find $\dfrac{dx}{du}$ – easy in this case

because $x = u + 1$ and $\dfrac{dx}{du} = 1$. So $dx = \dfrac{dx}{du} \times du = 1 \times du = du$

and our integral finally becomes:

$$\int \frac{u+1}{\sqrt{u}}\, du$$

which is the same as our other integral with u instead of x. We've already worked this out.

$$\int \frac{u+1}{\sqrt{u}}\, du \;=\; \frac{2}{3} u^{\frac{3}{2}} + 2u^{\frac{1}{2}} + C$$

Now we put back the variable we first thought of.

$$\int \frac{x}{\sqrt{x-1}}\, dx \;=\; \frac{2}{3} u^{\frac{3}{2}} + 2u^{\frac{1}{2}} + C \quad \text{where } u = x - 1$$

$$=\; \frac{2}{3}(x-1)^{\frac{3}{2}} + 2(x-1)^{\frac{1}{2}} + C$$

Note that when we've finished transforming the original integral, everything must be in terms of the new variable – we can't end up with something like:

$$\int x^2\,(1 + u)\, dx \quad \text{or} \quad \int \frac{1 + u^2}{x}\, du$$

We can, however, tolerate these mixtures of old and new while we're in the process of changing over: in fact, we shouldn't always be in too much of a hurry to substitute new for old – very frequently there can be cancellations or other simplifications. Let's have a look at an example of this.

Example   Find $\displaystyle \int x\sqrt{1 + 2x^2}\, dx$

Solution   Obviously we would like to simplify the function in the square root, so we put:

$$u = 1 + 2x^2$$

Now instead of worrying about putting the x to the left in terms of u, we'll go straight to dx. We know that d$x = \dfrac{dx}{du} \times du$, so we have to find $\dfrac{dx}{du}$.

To do this, we find $\dfrac{du}{dx}$ and turn it upside-down.

$$u = 1 + 2x^2 \quad \Rightarrow \quad \frac{du}{dx} = 4x$$

So: $\quad \dfrac{dx}{du} = \dfrac{1}{4x},$

and: $\quad dx = \dfrac{dx}{du} \times du = \dfrac{1}{4x} \times du$

We'll put what we've worked out into our original integral and see what still needs doing.

$$\int x \sqrt{1 + 2x^2} \; dx = \int x \times \sqrt{u} \times \frac{1}{4x} \times du$$

We can see that there is a cancellation in this case, and we have:

$$\int \frac{\sqrt{u}}{4} \; du = \int \frac{u^{\frac{1}{2}}}{4} \; du \quad = \quad \frac{1}{6} u^{\frac{3}{2}} + C$$

$$= \quad \frac{1}{6} (1 + 2x^2)^{\frac{3}{2}}, + C$$

when we put back the original variable.

Example Find $\displaystyle\int \frac{e^x}{(1 - 2e^x)^3} \; dx$

Solution Put $\quad u = 1 - 2e^x \qquad$ Then $\quad \dfrac{du}{dx} = -2e^x$

$$\frac{dx}{du} = -\frac{1}{2e^x}$$

$$\text{and} \quad dx = \frac{dx}{du} \times du = -\frac{du}{2e^x}$$

Our integral becomes: $\displaystyle\int \frac{e^x}{u^3} \times -\frac{du}{2e^x} = -\frac{1}{2} \int \frac{du}{u^3}$

$$= -\frac{1}{2} \int u^{-3} \; du$$

$$= \frac{1}{4} u^{-2} + C = \frac{1}{4u^2} + C$$

$$= \frac{1}{4(1 - 2e^x)^2} + C$$

Changing the limits

We'll have a look at a different set of examples, where a trigonometric substitution is used. Before we do this, a quick word about limits.
If there are limits on our original integral, i.e. if it's a definite integral, then we have to change the limits in accordance with our substitution. So for example with:

$$\int_0^1 x^4 (8 - 7x^5)^{\frac{2}{3}} \, dx$$

we would use the substitution $u = 8 - 7x^5$. The limits 1 and 0 refer to the x values. When $x = 1$, $u = 8 - 7 \times 1 = 1$ and when $x = 0$, $u = 8 - 7 \times 0 = 8$. The limits $x = 1$ and $x = 0$ are transformed to the limits $u = 1$ and $u = 8$ respectively – that is, the new limit occupies the same position as the corresponding old limit (even though this may mean the lower limit is larger than the upper, as in this case).

$$u = 8 - 7x^5 \quad \text{so} \quad \frac{du}{dx} = -35x^4, \quad \frac{dx}{du} = -\frac{1}{35x^4}$$

$$dx = \frac{dx}{du} \, du = -\frac{1}{35x^4} \, du$$

$$\int_0^1 x^4 (8 - 7x^5)^{\frac{2}{3}} \, dx \quad = \quad \int_8^1 x^4 u^{\frac{2}{3}} \left(-\frac{1}{35x^4}\right) du$$

$$= \quad -\frac{1}{35} \int_8^1 u^{\frac{2}{3}} \, du$$

$$= \quad \frac{1}{35} \int_1^8 u^{\frac{2}{3}} \, du \quad \text{By property of limits}$$

$$= \quad \frac{1}{35} \left[\frac{3}{5} u^{\frac{5}{3}}\right]_1^8$$

$$= \quad \frac{1}{35} \times \frac{3}{5} \times \left(8^{\frac{5}{3}} - 1^{\frac{5}{3}}\right)$$

$$= \quad \frac{3}{175} (32 - 1) = \frac{93}{175}$$

So when you use a substitution to evaluate a definite integral, remember you have to change three things:

1   the function you're integrating
2   the dx
3   the limits.

Note that, in the above example with a definite integral, we don't want to change back to the original variable.

You should now be able to answer Exercises 9, 10, 11, 12 and 13 on p. 78.

Trigonometric integration

You will need to repeatedly use the following three formulae so you should memorise them now.

$$\sin^2\theta + \cos^2\theta = 1$$

$$\cos 2\theta = \cos^2\theta - \sin^2\theta$$

$$\sin 2\theta = 2\sin\theta\cos\theta$$

From the first equation we can find either $\sin^2\theta$ or $\cos^2\theta$ in terms of the other and substitute this into the second equation to give:

$$\cos^2\theta = 1 - \sin^2\theta \qquad\qquad \sin^2\theta = 1 - \cos^2\theta$$

$$\Rightarrow \cos 2\theta = (1 - \sin^2\theta) - \sin^2\theta \quad\Rightarrow\quad \cos 2\theta = \cos^2\theta - (1 - \cos^2\theta)$$

$$= 1 - 2\sin^2\theta \qquad\qquad\qquad = 2\cos^2\theta - 1$$

These are useful formulae in their own right, but for integration purposes we rewrite them:

$$\sin^2\theta = \frac{1}{2}(1 - \cos 2\theta) \; ; \; \cos^2\theta = \frac{1}{2}(1 + \cos 2\theta)$$

θ can be any angle we like, so, for example:

$$\sin^2 5x = \frac{1}{2}(1 - \cos 10x) \text{ and } \cos^2\frac{y}{8} = \frac{1}{2}\left(1 + \cos\frac{y}{4}\right)$$

The advantage lies in transforming something involving a power, which can't be integrated immediately, into something involving a multiple angle, which can be integrated directly. We will now work through an example of this.

Evaluate: $\displaystyle\int_0^{\frac{\pi}{4}} \cos^2 4x \, dx$

Using our formula, we find that:

$$\cos^2 4x \quad = \quad \frac{1}{2}(1 + \cos 8x)$$

Our integral becomes:

$$\int_0^{\frac{\pi}{4}} \cos^2 4x \, dx \quad = \quad \int_0^{\frac{\pi}{4}} \frac{1}{2}(1 + \cos 8x) \, dx$$

$$= \quad \left[\frac{1}{2}\left(x + \frac{\sin 8x}{8}\right)\right]_0^{\frac{\pi}{4}}$$

$$= \quad \frac{1}{2}\left(\frac{\pi}{4} + \frac{\sin 2\pi}{8}\right)$$

$$= \quad \frac{\pi}{8} \quad (\text{since } \sin 2\pi = 0)$$

You should now be able to answer Exercise 14 on page 78.

Definite integrals

We saw that the formula for the area underneath a curve bounded by the two lines $x = x_2$ and $x = x_1$ and the x-axis is:

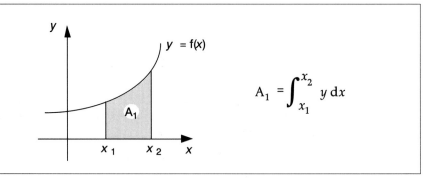

$$A_1 = \int_{x_1}^{x_2} y \, dx$$

If we wanted the area of the curve between the two lines $y = y_2$, $y = y_1$ and the y-axis, we need to swap everything round:

Figure 6.2

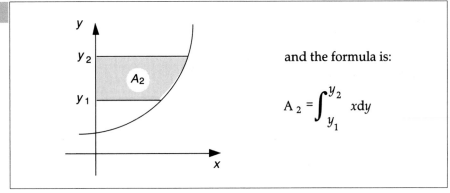

and the formula is:

$$A_2 = \int_{y_1}^{y_2} x\,dy$$

Note that if you are integrating with respect to y (that's the meaning of dy), the limits have to be the limits of y.

Let's have a look at an example of this.

Example   Find the area enclosed by the curve $y = x^2 + 2$, the lines $y = 6$, $y = 3$ and the y-axis.

Solution

Figure 6.3

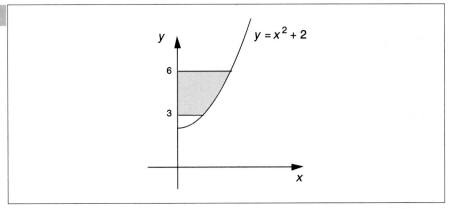

At the moment we have y given in terms of x: we have to rearrange this and make x the subject

$$y = x^2 + 2$$
$$x^2 = y - 2$$
$$x = \sqrt{y - 2}$$
$$= (y - 2)^{\frac{1}{2}} \quad \text{(taking the positive part since } x > 0\text{)}$$

The formula $A = \int_{y_1}^{y_2} x \, dy$ becomes:

$$A = \int_3^6 (y-2)^{\frac{1}{2}} \, dy = \left[\frac{2}{3}(y-2)^{\frac{3}{2}} \right]_3^6$$

$$= \frac{2}{3}\left(4^{\frac{3}{2}} - 1^{\frac{3}{2}} \right) = \frac{14}{3}$$

You should now be able to answer Exercise 15 on p. 79.

Areas between two curves

We can be asked to find the area enclosed between two curves: in this case we remember that the formula gives an area between the curve and the appropriate axis. We can then usually express the required area as the difference between two integrals.

Example   Find the points of intersection of the curve $y = x^2 + 2$ with the line $y = 3x$. Hence find the area enclosed between these two.

Solution   We draw a sketch first of all:

Figure 6.4

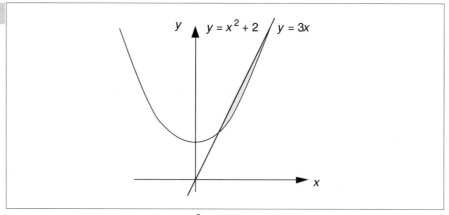

The curves intersect when $x^2 + 2 = 3x$

$$\Rightarrow \quad x^2 - 3x + 2 = 0$$

$$(x-2)(x-1) = 0$$

The area shaded in the sketch is found by finding the area underneath the line, which is:

$$\int_1^2 3x \, dx = P, \text{ say}$$

and subtracting the area underneath the curve,

$$\int_1^2 (x^2 + 2) \, dx = Q, \text{ say}$$

Figure 6.5

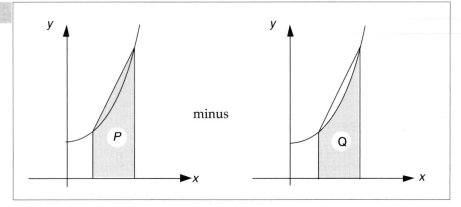

$$P = \int_1^2 3x \, dx = \left[\frac{3x^2}{2}\right]_0^2 = 6 - \frac{3}{2} = \frac{9}{2}$$

$$Q = \int_1^2 (x^2 + 2) \, dx = \left[\frac{x^3}{3} + 2x\right]_1^2 = \left(\frac{8}{3} + 4\right) - \left(\frac{1}{3} + 2\right) = \frac{13}{3}$$

The shaded region is then $\quad P - Q = \dfrac{9}{2} - \dfrac{13}{3}$

$$= \frac{27-26}{6} = \frac{1}{6}.$$

You should now be able to answer Exercise 16 on p. 79.

Volumes of revolution

Corresponding to the formulas for areas underneath curves are the formulas for calculating the volume when these areas are rotated around either axis. These are

$$V = \pi \int_{x_1}^{x_2} y^2 \, dx \qquad\qquad \text{[around the } x\text{-axis]}$$

and $\quad V = \pi \int_{y_1}^{y_2} x^2 dx \qquad\qquad \text{[around the } y\text{-axis]}$

Example   Find the volume swept out when the region bounded by the curve

$y = x^{\frac{1}{2}} e^x$, the x–axis and the ordinate $x = 1$ is rotated through an angle of 2π about the x-axis.

(Leave your answer in terms of π and e.)

Solution   We don't really have to know much about the shape of the curve; the important thing is that it starts at the origin, so the limits are 0 and 1.

Figure 6.6

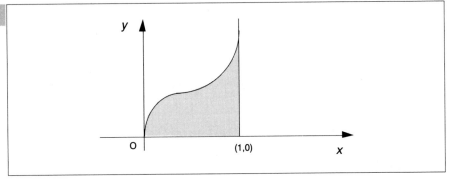

The volume is:

$$\int_0^1 \pi y^2 \, dx \;\; = \int_0^1 \pi \left(x^{\frac{1}{2}} e^x\right)^2 dx$$

$$= \pi \int_0^1 x e^{2x} \, dx$$

By parts: $\displaystyle\int_0^1 x e^{2x}$ $u = x$ $v^1 = e^{2x}$

                                   $u^1 = 1$ $v = \dfrac{1}{2} e^{2x}$

$$= \left[\dfrac{1}{2} x e^{2x}\right]_0^1 - \dfrac{1}{2} \int_0^1 e^{2x} \, dx$$

$$= \left[\dfrac{1}{2} x e^{2x} - \dfrac{1}{4} e^{2x}\right]_0^1 \;\; = \left(\dfrac{1}{2} e^2 - \dfrac{1}{4} e^2\right) - \left(-\dfrac{1}{4}\right)$$

$$= \dfrac{1}{4} + \dfrac{1}{4} e^2 = \dfrac{1}{4}(1 + e^2)$$

i.e. the volume is $\dfrac{\pi}{4}(1 + e^2)$

Here's an example where we have to split the volume into two sections.

Example	The diagram represents the circle $(x - 5)^2 + y^2 = 25$ and the straight line $2y = x$.
Figure 6.7	

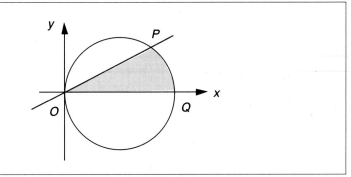

A toy top is obtained by rotating the shaded area OPQ through 360° about the *x*-axis. Calculate its volume.

Solution	We'll drop a perpendicular from P onto the *x*-axis, onto the point N, say
Figure 6.8	

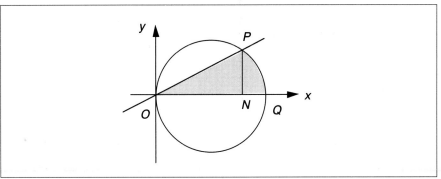

We can now find the separate volumes when the portions *OPN* and *PNQ* are rotated. To find the coordinates of *N*, we solve simultaneously:

$$(x - 5)^2 + y^2 = 25 \quad \ldots \text{①}$$
$$2y = x \quad \ldots \text{②}$$

② into ①　$(2y - 5)^2 + y^2 = 25$

$$4y^2 - 20y + \cancel{25} + y^2 = \cancel{25}$$
$$5y^2 - 20y = 0$$
$$5y\,(y - 4) = 0 \qquad \Rightarrow y = 0 \text{ or } y = 4$$

This gives $x = 8$ as the *x*-coordinate of *N*.

The volumes are then $\pi \int y^2 \, dx$, which gives:

$$\pi \int_0^8 \left(\frac{x}{2}\right)^2 dx \qquad \text{[This is area } OPN \text{ rotated]}$$

and

$$\pi \int_8^{10} [25 - (x-5)^2] \, dx \qquad \text{[since } x = 10 \text{ at } Q \text{, where } y = 0]$$

$$\pi \int_0^8 \left(\frac{x}{2}\right)^2 dx = \pi \int_0^8 \left(\frac{x^2}{4}\right) dx = \pi \left[\frac{x^3}{12}\right]_0^8 = \frac{128\pi}{3} \qquad \text{[A]}$$

$$\pi \int_8^{10} [25 - (x-5)^2] = \pi \int_8^{10} [25 - (x^2 - 10x + 25)] \, dx$$

$$= \pi \int_8^{10} (10x - x^2) \, dx = \pi \left[5x^2 - \frac{x^3}{3}\right]_8^{10}$$

$$= \pi \left\{\left(500 - \frac{1000}{3}\right) - \left(320 - \frac{512}{3}\right)\right\}$$

$$= \pi \left(\frac{500}{3} - \frac{448}{3}\right)$$

$$= \frac{52\pi}{3} \qquad \text{[B]}$$

This gives a total volume of $\dfrac{128\pi}{3} + \dfrac{52\pi}{3} = \dfrac{180\pi}{3} = 60\pi$

You should now be able to answer Exercises 17, 18 and 19 on p. 79.

Definite integration as the limit of the sum of rectangles

In this section we shall have a quick look at the way in which we can approximate an area by the sum of a series of rectangles. By decreasing the width of these rectangles we can get some idea of how their sum approaches the exact value that we could find by integration.

As an example, we'll take the particular area under the curve $y = \frac{1}{x}$ between the limits $x = 1$ and $x = 2$. As a preliminary, we divide the line between the x-coordinates to obtain subdivisions at $x = 1\frac{1}{4}$, $1\frac{1}{2}$ and $1\frac{3}{4}$. We then construct two sets of four rectangles, one set lying wholly above the curve and the other wholly beneath it. Consequently the area under the curve, A say, will be more than the sum of the areas of the first set and less than the sum of the areas of the second set.

Figure 6.9

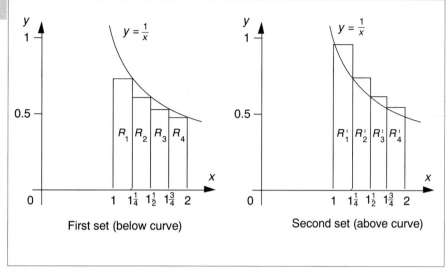

First set (below curve)   Second set (above curve)

We can work out that:

$$\sum_{i=1}^{4} = R_i = R_1 + R_2 + R_3 + R_4 = \frac{1}{5} + \frac{1}{6} + \frac{1}{7} + \frac{1}{8} \approx 0.63 \text{ (2 d.p.)}$$

and similarly:

$$\sum_{i=1}^{4} = R^1_i = \frac{1}{4} + \frac{1}{5} + \frac{1}{6} + \frac{1}{7} \approx 0.76 \text{ (2 d.p.)}$$

and so: $0.63 < A < 0.76$

We can increase the number of rectangles if we want to improve the accuracy: taking the number of strips to be n:

Table 6.1

Number of Rectangles	Lower Limit	Upper Limit
$n = 10$	0.67	0.72
$n = 100$	0.691	0.696
$n = 1000$	0.6929	0.6934

The actual value of the area, found by integration, is $\ln 2 = 0.69315$ (to 5 d.p.), which you can see is mid-way between the lower and upper limits.

You should now be able to answer Exercise 20 on p. 80.

EXERCISES

1   Integrate the following functions with respect to x and then differentiate your answer to check:

    a e^{2x} **b** $\sin 3x$ **c** $\cos 4x$ **d** $(1 - 3x)^5$

2   Find $\int x \sin 3x \, dx$.

3   Evaluate $\int_0^1 x \, e^{2x} \, dx$

4   Find **a** $\int x^2 \ln x \, dx$ **b** $\int x^2 \sin x$ (twice by parts)

5   Find $\int \ln x \, dx$ (Hint: write $\ln x$ as $\ln x \times 1$).

6   Find: $\int \dfrac{1}{(1 + x)(2 - x)} \, dx$

7   Evaluate: $\displaystyle\int_2^4 \dfrac{1}{2x^2 + x} \, dx$

8   Show that: $\displaystyle\int_0^4 \dfrac{11x^2 + 4x + 12}{(2x + 1)(x^2 + 4)} \, dx = \ln 675$

9   Find

    a $\int \dfrac{2x + 1}{x^2 + x + 1} \, dx$

    b $\int \tan x \, dx$

    (Hint: write as $\int \dfrac{\sin x}{\cos x} \, dx$)

10   Find: $\int x \sqrt{1 - x^2} \, dx$ Substitute $u = 1 - x^2$

11   $\int \dfrac{x^2}{(1 + 4x^3)^2} \, dx$ Substitute $u = 1 + 4x^3$

12   $\displaystyle\int_2^7 \dfrac{4x}{\sqrt{x + 2}} \, dx$ Substitute $u = x + 2$

13   $\displaystyle\int_e^{e^2} \dfrac{1}{x \ln x} \, dx$ Substitute $u = \ln x$

14   Find $\int \sin^2 3x \, dx$

15 Evaluate:

a $\displaystyle\int_0^2 x^4\,dx$ b $\displaystyle\int_{-1}^0 (x^3 - x)\,dx$ c $\displaystyle\int_0^{\pi/2} \sin x\,dx$ d $\displaystyle\int_0^1 e^{-x}\,dx$

e $\displaystyle\int_1^3 \frac{1}{1+x}\,dx$ (this will simplify)

16 Find the area enclosed by the curve $y = \dfrac{x}{x^2 + 1}$, the lines $x = 1$ and $x = 2$, and the x–axis.

17

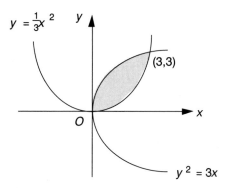

Calculate the area of the shaded region shown in the figure.

18 Find the equation of the chord which joins the points $A(-2, 3)$ and $B\,(0, 15)$ on the curve $y = 15 - 3x^2$.

   a   Show that the finite area enclosed by the curve and the chord AB is 4 square units.

   b   Find the volume generated when this area is rotated through 360° about the x-axis, leaving your answer in terms of π.

19 The diagram shows part of the graph of $y^2 = x - 1$. The region in the first quadrant bounded by the axes, the curve, and the line $y = 2$ is denoted by R. Find the volume of the solid generated when R is rotated through one revolution:

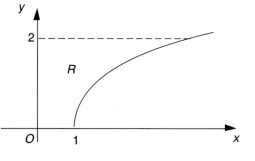

   a   about the y-axis

   b   about the x-axis.

20

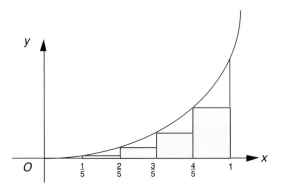

The diagram shows part of the curve $y = x^2$, with rectangles approximately the area under the curve between $x = 0$ and $x = 1$.

Prove that the total area of the four rectangles shown may be expressed as $\dfrac{1}{5^3} \left(\displaystyle\sum_{r=1}^{4} r^2 \right)$.

SUMMARY

We have studied ways by which we can integrate more complicated functions, including an introduction to integration by substitution which is a technique you will find very useful later on. You know also how to find the areas of more complicated regions, and the volumes that they generate when rotated.

7

First-order differential equations

INTRODUCTION
We can begin to use the skills we've acquired in integration to solve a type of equation that is met with very frequently when maths is used to model real-life situations. They are called differential equations and for the moment we shall only be looking at one particular kind that can be solved without any additional techniques.

Separating the variables

We have already learned how we can differentiate functions involving more than one variable. If we know, for instance, that:

$$x^2 + y^2 = 4x$$

then we can differentiate this with respect to x without too much difficulty, to get:

$$2x + 2y\frac{dy}{dx} = 4$$

rearrange:
$$2y\frac{dy}{dx} = 4 - 2x$$

$$\frac{dy}{dx} = \frac{4 - 2x}{2y} \qquad (\div 2y)$$

$$= \frac{2 - x}{y} \qquad (\div 2)$$

In this section we're going to study how we can reverse this process and find the original function knowing only the differential, i.e. in this case $\frac{dy}{dx} = \frac{2 - x}{y}$.

The equation connecting $\frac{dy}{dx}$ with the variables x and y can be more or less complicated; for the moment we shall be looking at a particular kind of equation, where we can separate the variables by division and multiplication. We want to arrive at an equation of the form $f(y)\frac{dy}{dx} = f(x)$.

Let's have a look at some examples and see which equations are of this type.

81

Examples

$$y \frac{dy}{dx} = x^2 (1 + y)$$

This is correct because we can divide both sides by $(1 + y)$ and finish with:

$$\frac{y}{1 + y} \frac{dy}{dx} = x^2$$

All the y's are on one side, with the x's on the other (we'll ignore $\frac{dy}{dx}$ for the moment), which is what we wanted.

$$\sin y \frac{dy}{dx} + x^2 = x^2 e^y$$

This doesn't look as though it's suitable, but in fact it's correct. After rearranging, we get:

$$\sin y \frac{dy}{dx} = x^2 e^y - x^2$$

$$= x^2 (e^y - 1) \qquad \text{factorising}$$

$$\frac{\sin y}{e^y - 1} \frac{dy}{dx} = x^2 \qquad \text{dividing by } (e^y - 1)$$

and again, each variable is confined to its particular side.

On the other hand, something like:

$$\frac{dy}{dx} = x + y$$

is not of this type. The addition sign means that we cannot separate the x and y.

Be careful with powers. They can be misleading. Given the equation:

$$e^{2x + y} \frac{dy}{dx} = x^2$$

you would be tempted to say that the $2x$ can't be separated from the y, which is not true. Remembering that powers are added, so that:

$$e^{2x + y} = e^{2x} \times e^y$$

and the equation can be written:

$$e^{2x} e^y \frac{dy}{dx} = x^2$$

$$e^y \frac{dy}{dx} = \frac{x^2}{e^{2x}} = x^2 e^{-2x}$$

You should now be able to answer Exercise 1 on p. 90.

Solving the equations

Not all of them are easy. You have to learn the tricks that help disguise them one way or another. Let's have a look now at ways of solving them, that is, to find what the function was before differentiation. The simplest case is probably where the function only involves x, as in:

$$\frac{dy}{dx} = x^2$$

We can quickly work out that this comes from:

$$y = \frac{x^3}{3} + C$$

noting that, as in the case of ordinary integration, we tag on an arbitrary constant. In fact, these constants have much more immediate importance than when we dutifully put them after our integration, so don't forget them.

When we have something like:

$$2y \frac{dy}{dx} = \sin x$$

we have to try and work out where the left-hand side came from.

Which function gives $2y \frac{dy}{dx}$ after differentiation with respect to x?

This way of looking at it can lead to confusion, so instead we integrate both sides with respect to x:

$$\int \left(2y \frac{dy}{dx}\right) dx \;\; = \int (\sin x)\, dx$$

and for the $\frac{dy}{dx} \times dx$, think of the dxs as 'cancelling', so that we can write:

$$\int 2y\, dy = \int \sin x\, dx$$

Each side can now be treated in the same manner, just as two normal functions to be integrated, and then we would have:

$$y^2 = -\cos x + C$$

Note that we only need one arbitrary constant even though we have two different integrations. Since the constants on each side are unknown, we can combine them to form one unknown constant. In fact, together with the differential equation, we are usually given limits, a pair of corresponding values for the variable, and from these we can work out the value of this constant. Suppose in the above example that $y = 2$ when $x = 0$. We put these values into our general solution and then:

$$2^2 = -\cos 0 + C$$
$$4 = -1 + C \Rightarrow C = 5$$

Having found C, we can rewrite our solution as:

$$y^2 = 5 - \cos x$$

We will have a look at one more example, and then you will be able to try some.

Example

The differential equation:

$$x\frac{dy}{dx} + \tan y = 0$$

where $x > 0$ and $0 < y < \frac{\pi}{2}$, satisfies the condition $y = \frac{1}{3}\pi$ when $x = 2$.

Show that the solution may be expressed in the form $x \sin y = k$, where k is a constant whose value is to be stated.

Solution

We'll rearrange the equation first of all:

$$x\frac{dy}{dx} = -\tan y$$

And again:
$$\frac{-1}{\tan y}\frac{dy}{dx} = \frac{1}{x}$$

Integrate both sides with respect to x:

$$\int \frac{-1}{\tan y}\frac{dy}{dx} \cdot dx = \int \frac{1}{x}dx$$

$$\int \frac{-\cos y}{\sin y}dy = \ln x$$

$$-\ln \sin y = \ln x + C \qquad \dots \text{①}$$

Now we'll put in the limits that are given, $y = \frac{\pi}{3}$ when $x = 2$

$$-\ln \sin \frac{\pi}{3} = \ln 2 + C$$

$$-\ln \frac{\sqrt{3}}{2} = \ln 2 + C$$

$$C = -\ln \frac{\sqrt{3}}{2} - \ln 2$$

$$= -\left[\ln \frac{\sqrt{3}}{2} + \ln 2\right] = -\left[\ln \sqrt{3}\right]$$

Putting our value for C back in the solution ①, we get:

$$-\ln \sin y \quad = \ln x - \ln \sqrt{3}$$

If we take $-\ln \sin y$ to the other side and combine, i.e.:

$$0 = \ln \frac{x \sin y}{\sqrt{3}}$$

$$\frac{x \sin y}{\sqrt{3}} = 1$$

then: $\quad x \sin y = \sqrt{3}$

which is in the form required, with $k = \sqrt{3}$.

Notice the fact that both the integrals involved ln – this is common.

You should now be able to answer Exercises 2, 3 and 4 on pp. 90–91.

Here is a typical example which involves lns, combining these and then giving y in terms of x as the final hurdle.

Example

Express $\dfrac{x}{(x + 1)(x + 2)}$ in partial fractions.

Solve the differential equation:

$$(x + 1)(x + 2) \frac{dy}{dx} = x(y + 1)$$

for $x > -1$, given that $y = \frac{1}{2}$ when $x = 1$. Express your answer in the form $y = f(x)$.

Solution

Note that the restriction on the values for x is to ensure that the denominator of the fraction:

$$\frac{x}{(x + 1)(x + 2)}$$

is never 0, which otherwise could lead to some strange results. Using partial fractions, we get that:

$$x \equiv A(x + 2) + B(x + 1)$$

$x = -2$ gives $B = 2$ and $x = -1$ gives $A = -1$, so that:

$$\frac{x}{(x + 1)(x + 2)} = \frac{2}{x + 2} - \frac{1}{x + 1} \qquad \dots ①$$

Rearranging the differential equation, we get:

$$\frac{1}{(y + 1)} \frac{dy}{dx} = \frac{x}{(x + 1)(x + 2)}$$

Integrating both sides with respect to x gives:

$$\int \frac{1}{y+1} \cdot \frac{dy}{dx} \cdot dx \;=\; \int \frac{x\,dx}{(x+1)(x+2)}$$

$$=\; \int \left(\frac{2}{x+2} - \frac{1}{x+1} \right) dx \quad \text{using } ①$$

Integrate:

$$\ln(y+1) = 2\ln(x+2) - \ln(x+1) + C \qquad \dots ②$$

Put in the limits of $y = \frac{1}{2}$ when $x = 1$:

$$\ln\frac{3}{2} \;=\; 2\ln 3 - \ln 2 + C$$

$$\ln\frac{3}{2} \;=\; \ln\frac{9}{2} + C$$

$$C \;=\; \ln\frac{3}{2} - \ln\frac{9}{2} = \ln\frac{1}{3}$$

and put this back into [2]:

$$\ln(y+1) \;=\; 2\ln(x+2) - \ln(x+1) + \ln\frac{1}{3}$$

$$\ln(y+1) \;=\; \ln\frac{(x+2)^2}{3(x+1)}$$

i.e.: $$y + 1 \;=\; \frac{(x+2)^2}{3(x+1)}$$

$$y \;=\; \frac{(x+2)^2}{3(x+1)} - 1$$

Then: $$y \;=\; \frac{x^2 + x + 1}{3(x+1)}$$

when we put both the terms together as one fraction.

Isolating y

In this example there was very little rearranging to present our solution for y in terms of x. It can happen that y occurs at the top and bottom of a fraction, something like:

$$\frac{y+2}{y-1} = x - 3$$

To isolate y, we first of all cross-multiply to clear all fractions:

$$y + 2 \;=\; (y-1)(x-3)$$

$$=\; yx - x - 3y + 3$$

Then we gather all terms containing y to one side, and all terms without y to the other:

$$y - yx + 3y = -x + 3 - 2$$
$$4y - yx = 1 - x$$

Then we can factorise the left-hand side,

$$y(4 - x) = 1 - x$$

and $\quad y = \dfrac{1 - x}{4 - x}$

You should now be able to answer Exercise 5 on p. 91.

Common mistakes

It takes some practice before you can combine terms involving lns accurately. Here are some examples of the more common types of error.

Error

$$\ln(y + 1) \quad = \quad 2\ln(x + 1) - \ln 3$$
$$\text{So:} \quad y + 1 = 2(x + 1) - 3$$
$$y \quad = \quad 2x - 2 \qquad \text{✘ Error}$$

This is not true.

All lns must be collected together to form one single ln before they can disappear.

Solution   Let's try that again:

$$\ln(y + 1) \quad = \quad 2\ln(x + 1) - \ln 3$$
$$= \quad \ln(x + 1)^2 - \ln 3$$
$$= \quad \ln\frac{(x + 1)^2}{3}$$

Then: $y + 1 = \dfrac{(x + 1)^2}{3}$

$$y = \frac{(x + 1)^2}{3} - 1$$

$$y = \frac{x^2 + 2x - 2}{3} \qquad \text{✔ Correct}$$

There are a couple of variations on the same basic theme:

Error

$$\ln(y + 1) = 3\ln x$$
$$\text{So:} \quad y + 1 = 3x$$
$$y = 3x - 1 \quad \dots \qquad \text{✘ Error}$$

Solution	There must be no figures outside the ln's.

Take the figure inside first, as in the example above:

$$\ln(y+1) = 3\ln x = \ln x^3$$

i.e.: $y + 1 = x^3$

$$y = x^3 - 1 \qquad \checkmark \text{ Correct}$$

Error	$\ln(y-1) \;=\; x^3 + 2$

So: $y - 1 = e^{x^3} + e^2 \dots$ ✗ **Error**

Solution	No. When we're putting each side as the power of e, we must take the whole side, so:

$$\ln(y-1) \;=\; x^3 + 2$$

and $y - 1 \;=\; e^{x^3 + 2} \;\Rightarrow\; y \;=\; e^{x^3 + 2} + 1$ ✓ **Correct**

The three types of error shown above are very common and you will need to be on your guard to avoid them.

Rates of change

There is one further topic that we have to cover while we're here. Occasionally, the differential equation is not given and you are expected to form it yourself from the data given. It very often involves rates of change of one or more variable, which in effect is the variable differentiated with respect to time. For example, the rate of change of a volume V is expressed $\dfrac{dV}{dt}$, or the rate of change of a radius r is written $\dfrac{dr}{dt}$.

There are two basic facts that you will need to set up a differential equation:

1   If the rate of change is increasing, it is positive, whilst a decrease means it is negative.

2   If a variable is proportional to some other variable, we express it as $k \times$ other variable, and use the limits given to evaluate k.

Let's have a look at a couple of examples of these.

Example	Express the following information in the form of a differential equation.

   a   The surface of a pond is partially covered with weed. The weed is increasing in area at a rate proportional to its area at that instant. (Call the area of the weed x m^2 and the growing time, t days).

b The rate at which the temperature, $\theta°$, of a body is decreasing is proportional to the difference between θ and the constant temperature of the medium, $\overset{o}{\theta}_m$

Solution

a The rate of change of the area of the weed is written $\dfrac{dx}{dt}$ and it's positive since it's increasing.

The differential equation is: $\dfrac{dx}{dt} = kx$

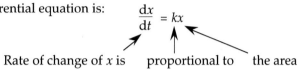

Rate of change of x is   proportional to   the area

b The rate of change of temperature, $\dfrac{d\theta}{dt}$, is negative since it's decreasing

i.e. $\dfrac{d\theta}{dt} = -k(\theta - \theta_m)$

Note that in both cases we used a constant of proportionality, k, which conventionally is taken to be positive. Here is another example where we set up and solve a differential equation.

Example

A vessel contains liquid which is flowing out from a small hole at a point O in the base of the vessel. At time t, the height of the liquid surface above O is z and the rate at which z is decreasing is inversely proportional to $z^{\frac{3}{2}}$.

Write down a differential equation which expresses $\dfrac{dz}{dt}$ in terms of z

Given that $z = 25$ when $t = 0$ and that $z = 16$ when $t = 30$, find the value of t when $z = 0$.

Solution

The rate of change of z, $\dfrac{dz}{dt}$, is negative since it's decreasing.

$$\dfrac{dz}{dt} = \dfrac{-k}{z^{\frac{3}{2}}} \qquad \ldots ①$$

Rearranging this, leaving the constant where it is:

$$z^{\frac{3}{2}}\,dz \quad = -k\,dt$$

i.e. $\displaystyle\int z^{\frac{3}{2}}\,dz \quad = -k\int dt \quad$ and integrating

$$\dfrac{2}{5}z^{\frac{5}{2}} \quad = -kt + C \qquad \ldots ②$$

Only one constant of integration is needed, but we already have another constant (k). To find the value of both these constants, we need *two* pairs of values for the variables which in fact we're given. Putting in the first of these pairs, i.e. $z = 25$ when $t = 0$

$$\frac{2}{5}(25)^{\frac{5}{2}} = 0 + C \implies C = \frac{2}{5} \times 5^5 = 2 \times 5^4 = 1250$$

we can rewrite ① as $\frac{2}{5}z^{\frac{5}{2}} = -kt + 1250$ ... ③

and substitute the second pair, i.e. $z = 16$ when $t = 30$

$$\frac{2}{5}(16)^{\frac{5}{2}} = -k(30) + 1250$$

$$\frac{2024}{5} = -30k + 1250$$

$$\implies 30k = 1250 - 404.8 = 845.2$$

$$\implies k = \frac{845.2}{30} = 28.173 \text{ (to 3 d.p.)}$$

Rewriting [3], we have:

$$\frac{2}{5}z^{\frac{5}{2}} \approx -28.173t + 1250 \qquad \text{... ④}$$

we want t when $z = 0$, so that

$$0 \approx -28.173t + 1250$$

$$t \approx \frac{1250}{28.173} \approx 44.4 \text{ (1 d.p.)}$$

You should now be able to answer Exercises 6 and 7 on p. 91.

EXERCISES

1 Decide whether the following differential equations belong to the 'variable separable' type.

a $\dfrac{dy}{dx} = 4xy$ **b** $\dfrac{dy}{dx} = \dfrac{\sin x}{\cos y}$ **c** $\dfrac{y}{x}\dfrac{dy}{dx} + 4 = 0y$ **d** $\dfrac{dy}{dx} = e^x - e^y y$

e $x\dfrac{dy}{dx} + y = 2y^2$ **f** $y\dfrac{dy}{dx} + xy^2 = x$ **g** $\dfrac{x}{y}\dfrac{dy}{dx} = x^2 + y^2 + x$

h $\ln x + \dfrac{dy}{dx} = \ln y$ **i** $y\dfrac{dy}{dx} = 2^{x-y}$ **j** $\sin^2 x\dfrac{dy}{dx} = \cos(x+y)$

2 Solve the differential equation: $\dfrac{dy}{dx} = y^2 e^{-2x}$

given that $y = 1$ when $x = 0$. Give your answer in a form expressing y in terms of x.

3 Given that: $\dfrac{dy}{dx} = -x^{\frac{1}{4}} y^2$

and that $y = \dfrac{5}{2}$ when $x = 0$, find the value of y when $x = 16$.

4 Given that x and y are positive, find the general solution of the differential equation:

$$\dfrac{dy}{dx} = -\dfrac{y}{x^2}$$

Show that the solution for which $y = e$ when $x = 1$ may be expressed in the form: $y = e^{\frac{1}{x}}$

5 Express y in terms of x, given that:

a $\dfrac{2y-1}{2y+1} = \left(\dfrac{x+3}{x-1}\right)$ **b** $\dfrac{y}{y+1} = \dfrac{e^{-x}}{1+e^{x}}$

6 A colony of bacteria increases at a rate proportional to its size. In 20 hours the size of the colony increases from 1500 to 3000. Formulate and solve a differential equation for the number N of bacteria at time t hours after the size was 1500

What size is the colony where $t = 80$?

How long did it take, to the nearest minute, for the size of the colony to increase from 2000 to 3000?

7 In a chemical reaction, hydrogen peroxide is converted into water and oxygen. At time t after the start of the reaction, the quantity of hydrogen peroxide that has **not** been converted is h and the rate at which h is decreasing is proportional to h. Write down a differential equation involving h and t. Given that $h = H$ initially, show that

$$\ln \dfrac{h}{H} = -kt, \qquad \text{where } k \text{ is a positive constant.}$$

In an experiment, the time taken for the hydrogen peroxide to be reduced to half of its original quantity was 3 minutes. Find, to the nearest minute, the time that would be required to reduce the hydrogen peroxide to one-tenth of its original quantity.

SUMMARY　　You have now seen how you can solve some simple models for naturally occurring phenomena: you also need to know how the raw solution for these can be changed into a more useful form, by the use of logarithms and algebraic manipulation.

Parameters

Sometimes it is more convenient to express the relationship between two variables with the aid of a third. This third variable is called the *parameter*. The two equations created (one linking the first variable to the parameter and the other linking the second variable to the parameter) are called *parametric* equations.

In this section we show you how to draw the graph of some parametric equations and how to eliminate the parameter if you wish to find the direct relationship between the two variables. Because of the complicated nature of the direct relationship it is often easier to keep the variables in their parametric form and operate on those equations. We shall see how we can extend the techniques we learnt for functions in cartesian form to include functions in parametric form: finding gradients, tangents and areas under curves for example.

Parametric equations

Suppose you ask two people to make up rules for transforming any number you care to give them.

One of them says: 'Double it and add 3.'

The other says: 'Multiply it by 3 and subtract 4.'

If t stands for your given number, and x and y for the results of the two transformations, then you can summarise what they said by writing:

$$x = 2t + 3 \quad \text{and } y = 3t - 4$$

For example, if you choose '3', then $x = 2 \times 3 + 3 = 9$ and $y = 3 \times 3 - 4 = 5$

if you choose '1', then $x = 5$ and $y = -1$

In fact, by choosing different values of t, you can make x have any value you like, or y have any value you like – but not both at the same time. They are related together by the variable t and are not free to change independently of each other. When t is used like this to define the relation between two other variables, we call it a *parameter*.

Sketching curves

There are two possible ways to sketch a curve given in parametric form. One of these is to look at the parametric equations, see what information they give, take some values for the parameter to get some particular points and plot these. If we take the equations we've just written, for example,

$$x = 2t + 3 \quad \text{and} \quad y = 3t - 4$$

we've already taken $\quad t = 3 \quad$ to give the point $(9, 5)$

$$\text{and} \quad t = 1 \quad \text{giving } (5, -1)$$

two more points, say $\quad t = 0 \quad$ giving $(3, -4)$

$$\text{and} \quad t = 2 \quad \text{giving } (7, 2)$$

should give us enough for our 'curve'.

Figure 8.1

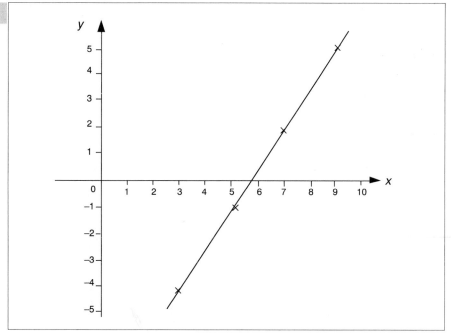

and we can see that it's a straight line. The second method is to find the corresponding cartesian equation by eliminating the parameter: we shall come to this shortly. For the moment, let's have a look at another example.

Example

Sketch the curve given by the parametric equations

$$x = t^2 - 1 \quad \text{and } y = 2t + 1$$

Solution   We'll find first of all the points where the curve crosses the axes. This will be when $x = 0 \Rightarrow t^2 - 1 = 0 \Rightarrow t = 1$ and $t = -1$. Putting these values in for y gives $y = 3$ and $y = -1$, giving the points $(0,3)$ and $(0,-1)$

$y = 0 \Rightarrow 2t + 1 = 0 \Rightarrow t = -\frac{1}{2}$. At this point, $x = (-\frac{1}{2})^2 - 1 = -\frac{3}{4}$, giving the point $(-\frac{3}{4}, 0)$

Looking at the function which defines x, we can see that x is an even function – there are two values of t (each giving a different value for y) which give the same value for x (for example, x is 8 for both $t = 3$ and $t = -3$). Also, the value of x can't be less than -1, and it reaches this minimum value when $t = 0$, in which case $y = 1$. It also increases in value much quicker than y, which is plodding along as a linear function to x's quadratic function. If we find a couple more points we can make a reasonable attempt at sketching the curve: $t = 3$ gives $(8,7)$ and $t = -3$ gives $(8,-5)$, so joining all these points we have:

Figure 8.2

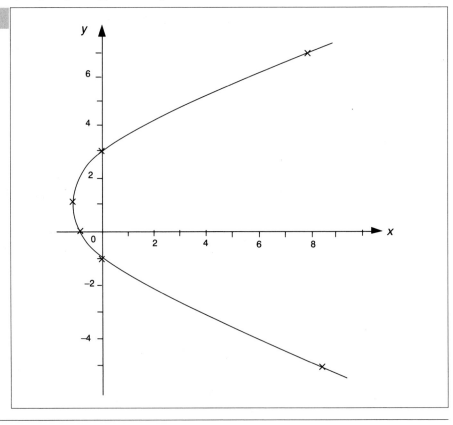

You should now be able to answer Exercise 1 on p. 99.

Eliminating the parameter

From the two parametric equations you can usually find the equation that connects x and y directly. In many cases you can do this by making the parameter t the subject of one of the parametric equations and substituting this into the other equation. Taking our first pair as an example, i.e.:

$$x = 2t + 3 \quad \text{and} \quad y = 3t - 4$$

we can rearrange the first of these to give

$$t = \frac{x - 3}{2}$$

and putting this into the second gives:

$$y = 3 \left(\frac{x - 3}{2}\right) - 4 = \frac{3x}{2} - \frac{9}{2} - 4 = \frac{3x}{2} - \frac{17}{2}$$

i.e. $\quad 2y = 3x - 17$

which is the corresponding *cartesian* equation.

The pair in the next example, $x = t^2 - 1$ and $y = 2t + 1$ are connected by rearranging the y-equation, $t = \frac{y - 1}{2}$, and putting this into the x-equation

$$x = \left(\frac{y - 1}{2}\right)^2 - 1 = \frac{y^2}{4} - \frac{y}{2} + \frac{1}{4} - 1$$

$$= \frac{y^2}{4} - \frac{y}{2} - \frac{3}{4}$$

i.e. $\quad 4x = y^2 - 2y - 3$

From this last example, you can start to see the advantage of using the parametric equations – they can be easier to deal with and quite often simplify calculations.

Sometimes squaring can help, especially with trigonometric functions. You can then use the relations $\sin^2 \theta + \cos^2 \theta = 1$, $1 + \tan^2 \theta = \sec^2 \theta$, etc., to eliminate t. For example,

if $\quad x = 2 \cos t \quad$ and $\quad y = 3 \sin t$

then $\quad \dfrac{x}{2} = \cos t \quad$ and $\quad \dfrac{y}{3} = \sin t$

$$\left(\frac{x}{2}\right)^2 = \cos^2 t \quad \text{and} \quad \left(\frac{y}{3}\right)^2 = \sin^2 t$$

and by adding, $\left(\dfrac{x}{2}\right)^2 + \left(\dfrac{y}{3}\right)^2 = \cos^2 t + \sin^2 t = 1$

There are also some algebraic pairs where squaring helps:

if $x = t + \dfrac{1}{t}$ and $y = t - \dfrac{1}{t}$

then $x^2 = t^2 + \dfrac{2t}{t} + \dfrac{1}{t^2}$ and $y^2 = t^2 - \dfrac{2t}{t} + \dfrac{1}{t^2}$

∴ $x^2 = t^2 + 2 + \dfrac{1}{t^2}$ ∴ $y^2 = t^2 - 2 + \dfrac{1}{t^2}$

Subtracting gives $x^2 - y^2$ $= \left(t^2 + 2 + \dfrac{1}{t^2}\right) - \left(t^2 - 2 + \dfrac{1}{t^2}\right)$

$$= 4$$

You should now be able to answer Exercises 2 and 3 on pp. 99–100.

Tangents and normals from parametric equations

To find the equation of a tangent or a normal to a curve, first of all we need to find the gradient of the curve or $\dfrac{dy}{dx}$ from our parametric equations.

Suppose these are $x = f(t)$ and $y = g(t)$ where f and g are functions of t. We differentiate these with respect to t

$$\frac{dx}{dt} = f'(t) \quad \text{and} \quad \frac{dy}{dt} = g'(t)$$

where the dash means differentiation (with respect to t)

$$\frac{dy}{dx} = \frac{dy}{dt} \times \frac{dt}{dx} \qquad \text{[We can think of the } dt\text{'s as 'cancelling']}$$

$$= \frac{dy}{dt} \div \frac{dx}{dt} \qquad \left[\text{since } \frac{dx}{dt} = \frac{1}{\frac{dt}{dx}}\right]$$

$$= \frac{\frac{dy}{dt}}{\frac{dx}{dt}} = \frac{g'(t)}{f'(t)}$$

Suppose, for example, that $x = 5t^2 + 2$ and $y = t^3 - t$. Differentiating them separately with respect to t,

$$\frac{dx}{dt} = 10t \text{ and } \frac{dy}{dt} = 3t^2 - 1$$

so $\dfrac{dy}{dx} = \dfrac{\frac{dy}{dt}}{\frac{dx}{dt}} = \dfrac{3t^2 - 1}{10t}$

Let's see how this works with one of the examples we've met already.

Example   Find the equation of the tangent to the curve given by $x = t^2 - 1$, $y = t - 1$ at the point where $t = 5$. Find also the equation of the normal.

Solution   We find $\dfrac{dx}{dt}$ and $\dfrac{dy}{dt}$ first of all.

$$\frac{dx}{dt} = 2t \quad \text{and} \quad \frac{dy}{dt} = 1$$

Then $\dfrac{dy}{dx} = \dfrac{\dfrac{dy}{dt}}{\dfrac{dx}{dt}} = \dfrac{1}{2t} = \dfrac{1}{10}$ when $t = 5$

Having found the gradient of the tangent, we can find the gradient of the normal by using:

$$(\text{Grad. tangent}) \times (\text{Grad. normal}) = -1$$

i.e.

$$\frac{1}{10} \times (\text{Grad. normal}) = -1$$

$$\text{Grad. normal} = -10$$

Now if we can find a point through which both the tangent and normal pass, we can find the equation of each of these. This is not too difficult – we put in the value $t = 5$ into both the parametric equations which gives:

$$x = 25 - 1 = 24 \text{ and } \quad y = 5 - 1 = 4$$

So the equation of the tangent is

$$y - 4 = \frac{1}{10}(x - 24) : \times \text{ by } 10$$

$$10y - 40 = x - 24$$

$$10y = x + 16$$

and the equation of the normal is

$$y - 4 = -10(x - 24)$$

$$y - 4 = -10x + 240$$

$$y + 10x = 244$$

In the second example, we are given parametric equations involving trigonometric functions:

Example   A curve is defined by the parametric equations:

$$x = \cos^3 t, \quad y = \sin^3 t, \quad 0 < t < \frac{\pi}{4}$$

Show that the equation of the normal to the curve at the point $P\ (\cos^3 t, \sin^3 t)$ is:

$$x \cos t - y \sin t = \cos^4 t - \sin^4 t$$

Solution   We want to find $\dfrac{dy}{dx}$, which means that we have to find $\dfrac{dx}{dt}$ and $\dfrac{dy}{dt}$.

From the given equations.

$$\frac{dx}{dt} = 3\ (\cos t)^2\ (-\sin t) \quad \text{and} \quad \frac{dy}{dt} = 3\ (\sin t)^2\ (\cos t)$$

Then $\dfrac{dy}{dx} = \dfrac{\frac{dy}{dt}}{\frac{dx}{dt}} = \dfrac{3 \sin^2 t \cos t}{-3 \sin t \cos^2 t} = -\dfrac{\sin t}{\cos t}$

We want the equation of the *normal*, so the gradient of this will be:

$$-\frac{1}{\frac{dy}{dx}} = \frac{\cos t}{\sin t}\ .$$

Usually we expect to be given a value for the parameter which specifies a particular point. In this case, however, the point given is a general point and consequently we have the general equation for the normal.

$$y - \sin^3 t = \frac{\cos t}{\sin t}\ (x - \cos^3 t)$$

× by $\sin t$ $y \sin t - \sin^4 t = x \cos t - \cos^4 t$

$\Rightarrow$ $x \cos t - y \sin t = \cos^4 t - \sin^4 t$

You should now be able to answer Exercises 4, 5, 6 and 7 on p. 100.

Areas under curves

If the area lies between the curve and the *x*-axis, so that we would use the formula:

$$\text{Area} = \int_{x_1}^{x_2} y\ dx$$

in cartesian coordinates, we can change the expressions involving x and y, including the limits in x, by substituting the parametric equations much as we would in finding any integral using the method of substitution.

In this connection, we have the important result:

$$\int_{x_1}^{x_2} y\,dx = \int_{t_1}^{t_2} y\,\frac{dx}{dt}\,dt$$

Suppose we had to find the area under the curve given by $x = t^2 - 1$, $y = 2t + 1$ which lies between the lines $x = 3$ and $x = 0$ and above the x-axis: we sketched the curve at the beginning of this section.

Figure 8.3

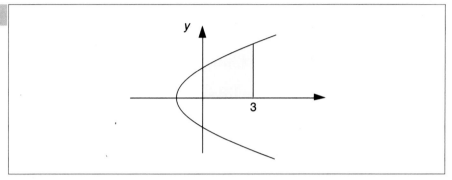

The limits $x = 3$ and $x = 0$, using $t = \sqrt{x + 1}$, become $t = 2$ and $t = 1$ (taking the positive values since the curve is above the x-axis).

y is simply replaced by $2t + 1$.

Since $x = t^2 - 1$, $\dfrac{dx}{dt} = 2t$ and the integral becomes:

$$\int_1^2 (2t + 1)\,2t\,dt \;=\; \int_1^2 (4t^2 + 2t)\,dt \;=\; \left[\frac{4t^3}{3} + t^2\right]_1^2$$

$$=\; \left[\left(\frac{32}{3} + 4\right) - \left(\frac{4}{3} + 1\right)\right] = \frac{37}{3}$$

We can also find the area by eliminating t for the corresponding cartesian equation.

You should now be able to answer Exercise 8 on p. 100.

EXERCISES

1 Sketch the curve given by the parametric equations:
   $x = 2t - 1$ and $y = t^2 + 1$

2 Find the cartesian equation corresponding to the following pairs of parametric equations by eliminating the parameter t:

   a $x = t + 1$, $y = t - 1$ **b** $x = 2t - 1$, $y = t^2 + 1$

   c $x = 2t$, $y = \dfrac{1}{t}$

3 Eliminate the parameter t from the following pairs of equations

   a $x = \cos t,$ $y = \sin t$

   b $x = \cos t - 1,$ $y = \sin t + 3$

   c $x = 3 \cos t + 2,$ $y = 3 \sin t + 1$

   d $x = 1 + \tan t,$ $y = 1 - \sec t$

   e $x = e^t + e^{-t},$ $y = e^t - e^{-t}$

   f* $x = \dfrac{t}{t+1},$ $y = \dfrac{t-1}{t}$ (*You don't have to square this one.)

4 Find the equation of the tangent to the curve:

    $x = t^2 + 1, \quad y = t^2 + t$ at the point where $t = 1$

5 Find $\dfrac{dy}{dx}$ when: $x = \dfrac{1+t}{1-t}$ and $y = \dfrac{1+2t}{1-2t}$

Show that $\dfrac{dy}{dx} = 2$ when $t = 0$ and find the equation of the normal to the curve at this point.

6 Find $\dfrac{dy}{dx}$ when: $x = \cos t, y = \cos t + \sin t$

7 The parametric equations of a curve are: $x = t + \sin t, y = 1 - \cos t$

Show that when $t = \dfrac{\pi}{2}, \dfrac{dy}{dx} = 1$, and use this to find the equation of the tangent to the curve at this point. The tangent crosses the x and y axes at P and Q respectively. Show that the area of $\triangle POQ$ is $\dfrac{\pi^2}{8}$, where O is the origin.

8 Find the area underneath the curve defined by $x = 4t, y = \dfrac{4}{t}$ and between the lines $x = 4$ and $x = 8$.

SUMMARY   We have been looking at another way of expressing the relationship between two variables: you need to be familiar with the correspondence between standard curves and their cartesian and parametric equations.

9

Geometry and curves

We shall be seeing how we can find angles and lengths in three dimensional objects – as an introduction to this we'll look at two rules which make solving triangles easier. After this we shall be looking at the graphs of some further functions: in particular, those which have the form of a fraction.

The sine and cosine rules

There are two rules that we can use to help us find additional information about a triangle when we already know some sides or angles. You may be familiar with them from some of your previous work, but if not, they are not difficult to apply.

The sine rule

The *sine rule* states that for any triangle, the ratio between each side and the sine of its opposite angle is the same, i.e.

Figure 9.1

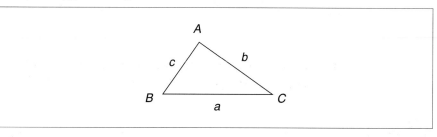

$$\frac{a}{\sin A} = \frac{b}{\sin B} = \frac{c}{\sin C} \qquad \text{[A]}$$

We can use this rule when we have information about any pair, i.e. any side and its corresponding opposite angle – otherwise we have to use the next rule, the cosine rule, which is a little more involved in the calculation. First let's have a look at an example using the sine rule.

101

Example   Using the usual notation for a triangle, find side a when $\angle B = 40°$, $\angle A = 60°$ and $b = 8$ cm.

Solution   Putting our values into [A],

$$\frac{a}{\sin 60°} = \frac{8}{\sin 40°}$$

i.e. $a = \dfrac{8 \times \sin 60°}{\sin 40°} = 10.8$ cm (to one decimal place)

Note that a is larger than b, because the $\angle A$ is larger than $\angle B$. In general, the largest side is opposite the largest angle.

Sometimes the information given can conceal the fact that there's a pair lurking somewhere – remembering that the angles of a triangle add up to 180° can reveal this.

Example   Find a when $\angle A = 50°$, $\angle C = 60°$, $b = 12$ cm

Solution   The missing angle is $180° - 50° - 60° = 70° = \angle B$

If we use the rule,

$$\frac{a}{\sin 50°} = \frac{12}{\sin 70°}$$

then $a = \dfrac{12 \times \sin 50°}{\sin 70°} = 9.8$ cm (to one decimal place)

There are also cases where more than one solution is possible. Suppose we were given the information that in a triangle, $a = 9$ cm, $b = 8$ cm and $\angle B = 60°$.

Figure 9.2

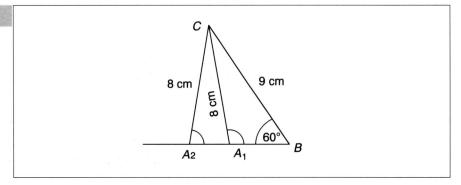

If we make a rough sketch of this, we see that we can draw two triangles satisfying the given conditions, $\triangle A_1BC$ and $\triangle A_2BC$. In the first of these, $\angle A_1$ is obtuse (greater than 90°) and in the second, $\angle A_2$ is acute (less than 90°). Let's find these two possible values for $\angle A$ and try to see how they arise. If we use the rule,

$$\frac{9}{\sin A} = \frac{8}{\sin 60°}$$

then $\quad \sin A = \dfrac{9 \times \sin 60°}{8} = 0.97428$

If I press inv sin 0.9743, my calculator produces an answer of 77.0 – but I know that this is not the only possible solution: the other is 180° – 77° = 103°, because sin is positive in the second quadrant.

So when we are working out an unknown angle, there are in general two solutions. Of course, if the first solution is 36°, the other will be 180° – 36° = 144°. We can disregard this second solution if we discover that the sum of this angle and one other known angle is more than 180°.

You should now be able to answer Exercises 1 and 2 on p. 116.

The cosine rule

We use this rule when we are given two sides and the included angle or three sides – the only disadvantage is that occasionally we may have to solve a quadratic to find a side: otherwise it is quite straightforward. Suppose we have a triangle ABC, with the perpendicular from A to BC drawn in, intersecting BC in X:

Figure 9.3

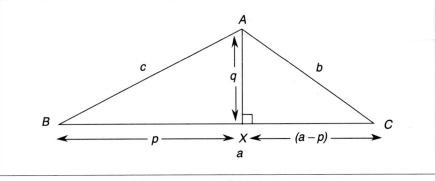

If BX is called p, XC will be $a - p$; AX we'll call q.

For $\quad \triangle ABX, \quad c^2 = p^2 + q^2 \qquad\qquad \ldots ①$

$\qquad\quad \triangle ACX, \quad b^2 = (a-p)^2 + q^2 \qquad \ldots ②$

$\qquad\qquad\qquad\quad = a^2 - 2ap + p^2 + q^2$

$\qquad\qquad\qquad\quad = a^2 - 2ap + c^2 \text{ (substituting ①)} \quad \ldots ③$

But from $\triangle AXB$, $\cos B = \dfrac{p}{c}$, i.e. $p = c \cos B$.

If we put this into [3]

$$b^2 = a^2 - 2a\,(c \cos B) + c^2$$

$$b^2 = a^2 + c^2 - 2ac \cos B \qquad \ldots \text{①}$$

If we'd taken any other vertex from which to draw our perpendicular, we would have ended up with either

$$a^2 = b^2 + c^2 - 2bc \cos A \qquad \ldots \text{②}$$
$$\text{or} \quad c^2 = a^2 + b^2 - 2ab \cos C \qquad \ldots \text{③}$$

and these three together form the equations for the cos rule. You can see that if any of the angles is 90°, the last term in one of the equations disappears, because $\cos 90° = 0$, e.g. if $\angle A = 90°$, from ②,

$$a^2 \;=\; b^2 + c^2 - 2bc \cos 90°$$
i.e. $\qquad a^2 \;=\; b^2 + c^2$

– which is our familiar Pythagoras's theorem. We'll have a look at an example of this.

Example	**a**	Find $\angle A$ when $a = 5$ cm, $b = 6$ cm, $c = 7$ cm.
	b	Find b when $a = 10$ cm, $c = 12$ cm, $\angle B = 60°$.

Solution   **a**   Using ②,

$$5^2 \;=\; 6^2 + 7^2 - 2.6.7.\cos A$$

so $\qquad \cos A \;=\; \dfrac{36 + 49 - 25}{84} \;=\; \dfrac{60}{84} \;=\; \dfrac{5}{7}$

so $\qquad A = 44.4°$ (to one decimal place)

b   Using ①,

$$b^2 \;=\; 10^2 + 12^2 - 2.10.12 \cos 60°$$
$$=\; 100 + 144 - 240 \times \dfrac{1}{2} \;=\; 124$$
$$b \;=\; 11.1 \text{ cm (to one decimal place)}$$

Bearings

You may already know that to find the bearing of B from A, you draw a north line at A, join AB and measure the angle between these lines.

Figure 9.4

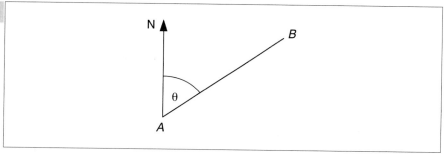

The angle θ is normally expressed in degrees, between $000°$ and $360°$. Here is an example of this.

Example

From a point P, A is at a distance of 8 km on a bearing of $340°$ and B is at a distance of 5 km on a bearing of $040°$. Find:

a   The distance AB

b   The bearing of B from A to the nearest degree.

Solution

Figure 9.5

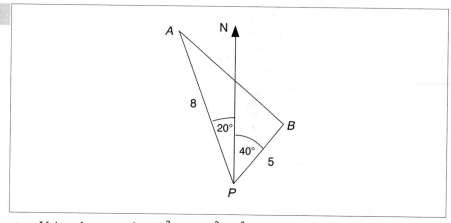

a   Using the cos-rule, AB^2 $= 8^2 + 5^2 - 2 \times 8 \times 5 \times \cos 60°$

$$= 89 - 40 = 49 \Rightarrow AB = 7 \text{ km}$$

b   Using the sine-rule, $\dfrac{\sin A}{5} = \dfrac{\sin 60°}{7} \Rightarrow A = 38°$ (nearest)

The bearing of B from A is then $180° - 58° = 122°$

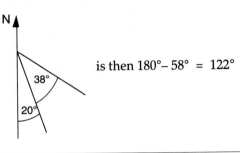

You should now be able to answer Exercises 3 and 4 on p. 116.

With these techniques, we can see how we can find angles and lengths in three dimensions.

Coordinate geometry in three dimensions

We find the coordinates of a point relative to a framework of 3 axes in much the same way as in two dimensions: so many along (x), so many back (y) and so many up (z). Distances are also a logical extension from two dimensions: if two points have coordinates (x_1, y_1, z_1) and (x_2, y_2, z_2) the distance between them is given by:

$$\sqrt{(x\text{-diff})^2 + (y\text{-diff})^2 + (z\text{-diff})^2} \quad \text{i.e.} \quad \sqrt{(x_2 - x_1)^2 + (y_2 - y_1)^2 + (z_2 - z_1)^2}$$

Example

Figure 9.6

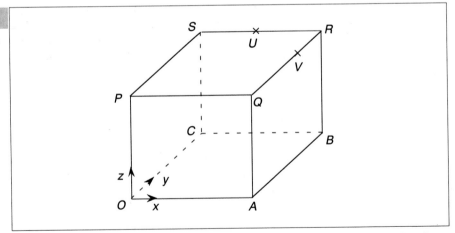

In the rectangular box in the diagram, $OA = 4$, $OC = 3$ and $OP = 5$. U is the mid-point of the line joining SR, V is the point on QR such that $QV = 2VR$.

Given that the x, y and z axes are in the direction of OA, OC and OP respectively, give the coordinates, relative to the origin O, of each of the points A, B, C, P, Q, R, S, U and V.

Find also the length of the line CV.

Solution   The coordinates are $A(4, 0, 0)$, $B(4, 3, 0)$, $C(0, 3, 0)$, $P(0, 0, 5)$, $Q(4, 0, 5)$, $R(4, 3, 5)$, $S(0, 3, 5)$, $U(2, 3, 5)$, $V(3, 2, 5)$

The distance CV is $\sqrt{3^2 + 1^2 + 5^2} = \sqrt{35}$

Geometry in three dimensions

When we are in three dimensions, we deal with *planes*, which are flat surfaces like the top of a table and *lines*. Both of these can be twisted round at any angle and so to solve problems involving them we have to be able to find the angle between:

a   a line and a plane
b   two planes
c   two lines.

In general we have to find, or make, a suitable triangle and then use either basic trigonometry for a right-angled triangle or the cos/sin rules for any other triangle.

This section looks at each of the cases in turn.

A line and a plane

Our triangle in this case comes from choosing a point on the line and dropping a perpendicular onto the plane from this point. Then the portion of the line from the plane to the point, the perpendicular and the 'shadow' of the line onto the plane (called the *projection*) make up our triangle:

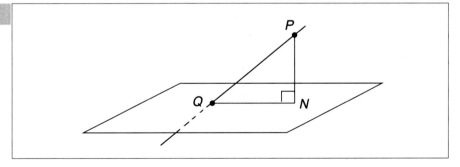

Here Q is the point where the line crosses the plane, P is a point on the line, PN is the perpendicular from P onto the plane, and QN is the 'shadow' or projection of the line onto the plane.

Let's see how this works with a couple of examples.

Example	A cuboid has a square base of 5 cm and a height of 2 cm. Find the angle between the line joining opposite corners and the base.

Solution	Firstly, a diagram:

Figure 9.8

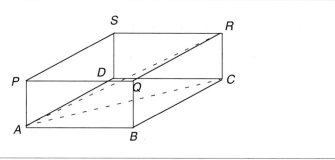

In the diagram, we've taken the opposite corners A and R, and we want to find the angle between AR and the base. In this case we already have a very convenient triangle, since RC is in fact a perpendicular onto the base $ABCD$. So we identify our triangle ARC and redraw this to find the angle we want, which is $R\hat{A}C$:

Figure 9.9

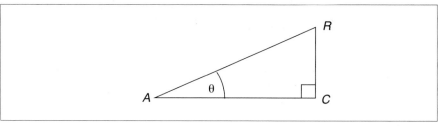

Now we need some lengths, although since it is a right-angled triangle, two will do. We're given the height RC as 2 cm so we have just to find AC. We can find this by taking a bird's-eye view of the base:

Figure 9.10

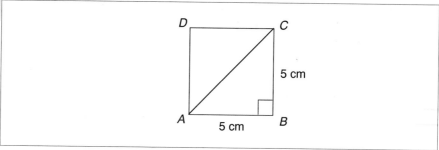

This comes from Pythagoras :

$$AC^2 = 5^2 + 5^2 = 50$$

so $AC = \sqrt{50}$ cm $= 5\sqrt{2}$ cm

We can now mark these on our triangle and find θ:

Figure 9.11

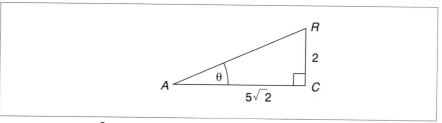

$$\tan \theta = \frac{2}{5\sqrt{2}} \quad \Rightarrow \quad \theta = 15.8° \text{ (1 d.p.)}$$

Example   A tetrahedron has a horizontal equilateral triangular base of side 6 cm and the sloping edges are each of length 4 cm. Find the inclination of a sloping edge to the horizontal.

Solution   We'll have a look at a diagram:

Figure 9.12

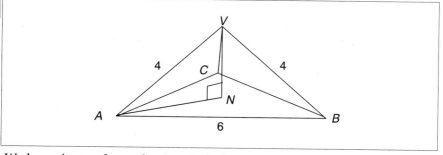

We haven't a ready-made triangle in this case, so we drop a perpendicular from V, the vertex, onto the base. We're going to use the triangle VAN, where N is the foot of the perpendicular, and so we need the length of AN. Looking from the top:

Figure 9.13

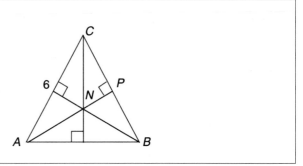

N is the 'centre' of the triangle which is one-third of the way up from a base, so that for example $PN = \frac{1}{3}PA$. Since *ABC* is an equilateral triangle, *CP* is half of the base *CB*, i.e. $\frac{1}{2}$ of 6 cm = 3 cm. Then we can find *AP* from Pythagoras:

$$AC^2 = AP^2 + CP^2$$
$$6^2 = AP^2 + 3^2 \;\Rightarrow\; AP = \sqrt{27} \;=3\sqrt{3}$$

Since *AN* is $\frac{2}{3}AP$, $AN = 2\sqrt{3}$ cm.

We can now draw our final triangle:

Figure 9.14

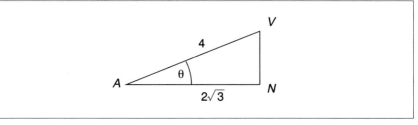

and the required angle θ is given by:

$$\cos\theta = \frac{2\sqrt{3}}{4} = \frac{\sqrt{3}}{2} \Rightarrow \theta = 30°$$

Two planes

The method in this case sounds more complicated than it actually is. We have to choose a point on the line where the two planes meet and draw perpendiculars along each of the planes from this point. The angle between these perpendiculars is the angle we're after and usually a suitable triangle will be obvious. Let's see how this works.

| **Example** | A tetrahedron has all its edges of length 6 cm. Find the angle between two adjacent faces. |

| **Solution** | |

| **Figure 9.15** | 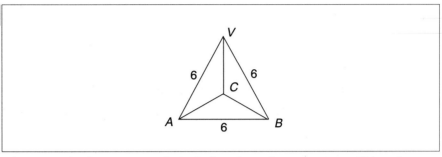 |

If we take the faces *VAB* and *VAC*, their line of intersection is *VA* and we want to choose a point on *VA* to put a perpendicular across each face. Since both the triangles *VAB* and *VAC* are equilateral this is quite straightforward since we can take the mid-point*, which we can call *P*:

(*This is not always the case with other triangles.)

| **Figure 9.16** | 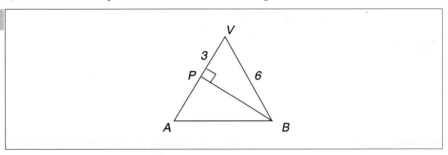 |

As in the previous example, $PB = 3\sqrt{3}$.

We repeat this process with the triangle *VAC*, where *PC* is conveniently also perpendicular to *VA*, and re-draw the diagram:

| **Figure 9.17** | 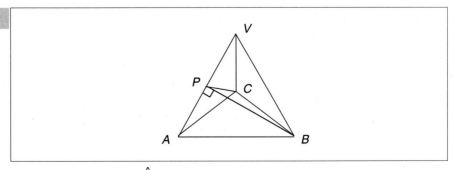 |

The angle we need is $B\hat{P}C$, so we extract the triangle *BPC*.

Figure 9.18

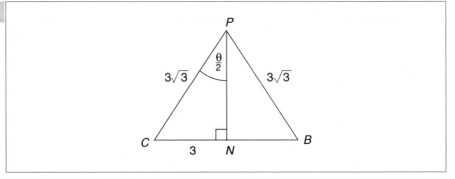

Since $PC = PB = 3\sqrt{3}$, the triangle BPC is isosceles and N will bisect the base, so that $CN = 3$. $C\hat{P}N$ is half the angle we want, so that:

$$\sin C\hat{P}N = \frac{3}{3\sqrt{3}} \Rightarrow C\hat{P}N = 35.26°$$

This gives CP, the required angle, as 70.5° (1 d.p.)

You should now be able to answer Exercises 5, 6 and 7 on p. 117.

Curve sketching

By taking a few sample points we can form an idea of the general shape of a curve. However there are certain points that are of more interest to us than others. Some functions have asymptotes – lines towards which the function tends as one of the variables tends toward infinity (∞). We want to look out for these, for points where the line crosses either the x-axis or the y-axis and also for turning points which we can find by differentiating.

A systematic approach

We shall generally be more interested in the shape of the curve than accurately plotted points (although for some topics we shall be using the detailed approach). There are some questions we can ask that allow us to determine the most important feature of a curve in a fairly systematic fashion. Let's have a look at these and see how they apply to sketching a typical curve, say:

$$y = \frac{x + 1}{x - 1}$$

Question 1: x on the bottom

Does the function contain a fraction with a function of x on the bottom? (If the answer is no, go straight to Question 4.)

In this case the answer is 'yes', since $(x - 1)$ is on the bottom, so we continue to the next question.

Question 2: Asymptotes on the x-axis

For what value(s) of x is this function zero?

This will be $x = 1 : x$ is not allowed to take this value, since fractions with zero on the bottom are infinitely large (try working out $\frac{2}{0}$ on your calculator). We express this fact by drawing in a dotted line at $x = 1$ and calling it an *asymptote*.

Question 3: Asymptotes on the y-axis

As x increases, does y tend to a definite value? (If y increases indefinitely, go on to the next question.)

For our curve, as x becomes large, y goes closer and closer to 1 – you can try this yourself by putting in the values of $x = 10$; 100; and 1000 and seeing what values of y you obtain. No matter how large a value of x you substitute, you can never actually find y to be exactly 1, although you can get as close as you like. This is another *asymptote* marked with another dotted line, this time at $y = 1$.

Question 4: Points on the axes

Where does the curve cross the axes?

We can find these points by substituting first $x = 0$ and then $y = 0$.

If $x = 0$, $y = \dfrac{+1}{-1} = -1$

If $y = 0$, $\dfrac{x + 1}{x - 1} = 0$ $\Rightarrow x = -1$

Question 5: Turning points

Are there any turning points?

You can work this out using the techniques we covered for finding maxima and minima in Module P1, Section 8, *Differentiation* but for the time being we will look at curves that have no turning points – we shall come back to curves which have turning points at the end of this section.

Question 6

Is y positive or negative either side of the x-asymptote(s)?

The point is that the 'forbidden' value of x creates a gap in the curve called a *discontinuity*. In our example, where $y = \dfrac{x + 1}{x - 1}$, if x is slightly less than 1, say $x = 0.99$, y will be negative (and large) and if x is slightly greater than 1, say $x = 1.01$, y will be positive (and large). So across the gap, where $x = 1$, the curve leaps from the bottom to the top. (Have a look at Figure 9.20 and this might make it clearer.)

To find out whether the curve comes down from the top or up from the bottom we substitute values of x slightly less than and slightly more than the critical value of the asymptote and see whether the corresponding value of y is positive or negative.

The sketch

Let's collect the information that we've found so far:

- Asymptotes at $x = 1$ and $y = 1$
- Crosses axes at $(0, -1)$ and $(-1, 0)$
- No turning points
- Positive above the x-asymptote, negative below.

This is actually enough to sketch the curve.

Drawing the axes and marking in this information, as in Figure 9.19:

Figure 9.19

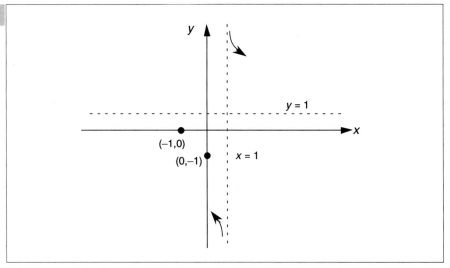

Then, remembering that the curve tends to $y = 1$ as x gets larger, we can fill in the rest:

Figure 9.20

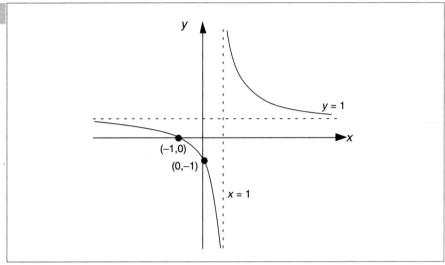

Turning points

We'll have a look now at a curve with a turning point.

Example Sketch the graph of $y = x^3 - 3x$.

Solution We differentiate, $\dfrac{dy}{dx} = 3x^2 - 3 = 0$ for the turning points.

$$3x^2 - 3 = 0 \Rightarrow x = \pm 1$$

$\dfrac{d^2y}{dx^2} = 6x$ so when $x = 1$, $y = -2$ and $\dfrac{d^2y}{dx^2} > 0$ MINIMUM

when $x = -1$, $y = 2$ and $\dfrac{d^2y}{dx^2} < 0$ MAXIMUM

when $x = 0$, $y = 0$
when $y = 0$, $x^3 - 3x = 0 \Rightarrow x(x^2 - 3) = 0$
$$\Rightarrow x = 0 \text{ or } x = \pm \sqrt{3}$$

y is an *odd* function: it has 180° rotational symmetry. The curve looks something like the one shown in Figure 9.21.

Figure 9.21

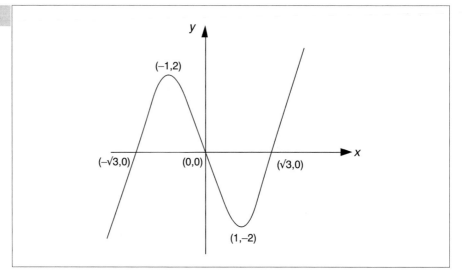

You should now be able to answer Exercises 8, 9, 10 and 11 on p. 118.

EXERCISES

1   Using standard notation, find a (to one decimal place) when:

   a $\angle A = 40°$, $\angle B = 70°$, $b = 12$ cm

   b $\angle A = 38°$, $\angle B = 72°$, $c = 15$ cm

2   Find $\angle A$ when:

   a $a = 11$ cm, $b = 10$ cm, $\angle B = 50°$

   b $a = 2$ cm, $b = 5$ cm, $\angle B = 40°$

3   Find $\angle A$ when:

   a $a = 9$, $b = 8$, $c = 7$

   b $a = 4$, $b = 3$, $c = 2$ (cos is negative-angle in second quadrant)

4   Find a when:

   a $b = 2$, $c = 5$, $\angle A = 21.5°$

   b $b = 4$, $c = 5$, $\angle A = 115°$

5

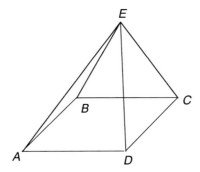

The figure shows a square-based pyramid in which:

$$AB = BC = CD = DA = AE = BE = CE = DE.$$

Find the angles between:

a   the lines *AE* and *CD*

b   the line *AE* and the plane *ABCD*

c   the planes *ABE* and *ABCD*.

6 A pyramid has a horizontal rectangular base *ABCD* with *AB* = 12 cm and *BC* = 5 cm.

The vertex *V* is vertically above *A* and *VB* = 20 cm. Calculate, to the nearest degree:

a   the angle between the planes *VCD* and *ABCD*

b   the angle between the skew lines *VC* and *AB*.

7 A pyramid has a square base *ABCD* of side *a* and its vertex is *E*. Each sloping face makes an angle 60° with the base.

a   Find the height of the pyramid.

b   Find the length of each sloping edge.

c   Find the angle between each sloping edge and the base.

d   Show that:

$$\sin E\hat{A}B = \frac{2}{\sqrt{5}}$$

P is a point on *BE* such that *AP* and *CP* are both perpendicular to *BE*.

e   Calculate the length of *AP*.

f   Show that the angle between adjacent sloping faces is $\cos\left(-\frac{1}{4}\right)$.

8 Find the values of x at which the graphs of the following functions have asymptotes:

a $y = \dfrac{1}{x-1}$ **b** $y = \dfrac{x}{x+1}$ **c** $y = \dfrac{x+2}{(x-1)(x+4)}$ **d** $y = \dfrac{x}{x^2-x-6}$

9 For each of the four functions above, state the value that y tends to as x increases (this is the *y-asymptote*).

10 Sketch the graphs of:

a $y = \dfrac{1}{x-1}$ **b** $y = \dfrac{x}{x+1}$ **c** $y = \dfrac{2-x}{2+x}$ **d** $y = \dfrac{3+2x}{2-3x}$

11 Find the turning points of the function $f(x) = \dfrac{x}{1+x^2}$.

Sketch the curve $y = f(x)$.

SUMMARY

In this section we have studied two different facets of geometry: in the three dimensional work we have seen how we can reduce a problem in 3D to one in 2D if we take an appropriate slice through the figure. Once we have done this, we have the available techniques to solve the resulting triangle. We have also extended the range of curve families we can sketch to include those with discontinuities where the value of the function increases indefinitely.

10

Binomial expansion

INTRODUCTION When expanding an expression like $(a + b)^2$ we know that in addition to $a^2 + b^2$ there is a middle term, $2ab$, i.e. $(a + b)^2 = a^2 + 2ab + b^2$. In more complicated expressions, these 'middle terms' have a pattern of their own. In this section we will learn how we can use this pattern to devise a formula by which we can work out any of these middle terms that we need. We shall then have a look at some typical exam questions and their methods of solution.

Pascal's triangle

One way of expanding $(1 + x)^6$ would be to write it as:

$$(1 + x)^6 = (1 + x)(1 + x)(1 + x)(1 + x)(1 + x)(1 + x)$$

and multiply it out, bracket by bracket. Even using short-cuts, this would still take some time – it would be better to have a general formula that would give us the result we want quite quickly.

To find this general formula, we look at the first five expansions of $(1 + x)^n$ – when $n = 1, 2, 3, 4, 5$ say – and see if we can find a pattern emerging. We then have to convert this pattern into a formula with which we can predict expansions with larger values of n.

So let's start with these first few expansions

$n = 1$: $(1 + x)^1$ $\qquad\qquad = 1 + x$

$n = 2$: $(1 + x)^2 = (1 + x)(1 + x)$ $\quad = 1 + x + x + x^2$ $\qquad\qquad = 1 + 2x + x^2$

$n = 3$: $(1 + x)^3 = (1 + x)^2(1 + x)$ $\quad = 1 + 2x + x^2 + x + 2x^2 + x^3$ $\qquad = 1 + 3x + 3x^2 + x^3$

$n = 4$: $(1 + x)^4 = (1 + x)^3(1 + x)$ $\quad = $ etc. $\qquad\qquad\qquad\qquad = 1 + 4x + 6x^2 + 4x^3 + x^4$

$n = 5$: $(1 + x)^5 = (1 + x)^4(1 + x)$ $\quad = $ etc. $\qquad\qquad\qquad\qquad = 1 + 5x + 10x^2 + 10x^3 + 5x^4 + x^5$

There is a pattern starting to form – at least for some of the coefficients. We can see that the coefficients are symmetrical about the middle – so let's rewrite our expansions in such a way that this symmetry is more evident. We can also take the coefficients only and leave out the powers of x:

119

$n = 0$						1						
$n = 1$					1		1					
$n = 2$				1		2		1				
$n = 3$			1		3		3		1			
$n = 4$		1		4		6		4		1		
$n = 5$	1		5		10		10		5		1	

You can see that for completeness we have included the case where $n = 0$ (anything to the power zero is 1, so $(1 + x)^0 = 1$). This way of writing it was devised by the French mathematician Pascal and so it's called *Pascal's triangle*. The pattern is that any number is the sum of the two numbers above it – we can now calculate the coefficients of $(1 + x)^6$ by taking the last line of our triangle and adding them in pairs:

1	$(1 + 5)$	$(5 + 10)$	$(10 + 10)$	$(10 + 5)$	$(5 + 1)$	1

that is   1   6   15   20   15   6   1

and so $(1 + x)^6 = 1 + 6x + 15x^2 + 20x^3 + 15x^4 + 6x^5 + x^6$

The pattern is the first step to finding a formula – in itself it's of little use for predicting the coefficients of $(1 + x)^{20}$, we'd have to complete the triangle for all the steps in between which would be both tedious and time consuming. A formula on the other hand is more flexible, giving us the precise coefficient that we want for any value of n – but of course it's correspondingly more difficult to discover.

General coefficients

Luckily a formula has been worked out. It would probably take quite a while before we saw the relationship between the power and the coefficients, between (taking the last example):

6   and   1, 6, 15, 20, 15, 6, 1

Apart from the 1 at the beginning and the 1 at the end, the relationship is

$$1, 6 = \frac{6}{1}, \quad 15 = \frac{6 \times 5}{2 \times 1}, \quad 20 = \frac{6 \times 5 \times 4}{3 \times 2 \times 1}, \quad 15 = \frac{6 \times 5 \times 4 \times 3}{4 \times 3 \times 2 \times 1}, \quad 6 = \frac{6 \times 5 \times 4 \times 3 \times 2}{5 \times 4 \times 3 \times 2 \times 1}, 1$$

which can be written, using our knowledge of factorials:

$$1, \quad 6 = \frac{6!}{5!1!}, \quad 15 = \frac{6!}{4!2!}, \quad 20 = \frac{6!}{3!3!}, \quad 15 = \frac{6!}{2!4!}, \quad 6 = \frac{6!}{1!5!}, \quad 1$$

If we now define 0! to have the value 1, we can write the two 1s at either end as:

$$\frac{6!}{6!0!} \quad \text{and} \quad \frac{6!}{0!6!} \quad \text{respectively}$$

and our coefficients could be written:

$$\frac{6!}{6!0!}, \frac{6!}{5!1!}, \frac{6!}{4!2!}, \frac{6!}{3!3!}, \frac{6!}{2!4!}, \frac{6!}{1!5!}, \frac{6!}{0!6!}$$ (Remember that 0! is defined to be 1.)

Can you see the pattern? If we want the coefficient of x^r in $(1 + x)^6$, we work out:

$$\frac{6!}{(6-r)!r!}$$

Now check that this gives the correct coefficient when $r = 1, 3$ and 5.

To make the formula even more flexible, we can say that the coefficient of x^r in $(1 + x)^n$ is:

$$\frac{n!}{(n-r)!r!}$$

This is written ^nC_r or $\binom{n}{r}$. You could well find that it is a function on your calculator.

Let's check this with a couple of examples:

The coefficient of x^2 in $(1 + x)^3$ is (here $r = 2$ and $n = 3$)

$$\frac{3!}{1!2!} = \frac{3 \times 2 \times 1}{1 \times 2 \times 1} = 3,$$ and checking back we see this is the correct answer.

The coefficient of x^3 in $(1 + x)^5$ is (here $r = 3$ and $n = 5$)

$$\frac{5!}{2!3!} = \frac{5 \times 4 \times 3 \times 2 \times 1}{2 \times 1 \times 3 \times 2} = 10,$$ which is the coefficient we calculated earlier.

This means that we can write down the general expansion of $(1 + x)^n$, where n is any integer, as:

$$(1 + x)^n = 1 + \binom{n}{1}x + \binom{n}{2}x^2 + \binom{n}{3}x^3 + \dots + \binom{n}{n-1}x^{n-1} + x^n$$

You should now be able to answer Exercise 1 on p. 126.

More complex expansions

It can happen that instead of $(1 + x)^n$ we have something like $(1 + 2x)^n$ or $(1 - x)^n$ but this doesn't drastically change the expansion. We just replace any x in the terms with $2x$ and $-x$ respectively. So the term in x^4 in the expansion of $(1 + 2x)^7$ is:

$$\frac{7!}{3!4!}(2x)^4 = \frac{7 \times 6 \times 5}{3 \times 2 \times 1} \times 16x^4 = 560x^4$$

The coefficient of x^3 in the expansion of $(1 - x)^5$ is given by:

$$\frac{5!}{2!3!}(-x)^3 = \frac{5 \times 4}{2 \times 1} \times -x^3 = -10x^3$$

This is the term with x^3. Since we've only asked for the coefficient of x^3, the answer is -10.

We can also have series where the first term in the bracket is not 1 – in this case the general expansion is:

$$(a + b)^n = a^n + \binom{n}{1} a^{n-1} b^1 + \binom{n}{2} a^{n-2} b^2 + \ldots + \binom{n}{n-1} ab^{n-1} + b^n$$

Note that the power of a decreases by 1 and the power of b increases by 1 each time, so that the sum of these powers is constant, n in fact.

Also, when only a few terms of the expansion are asked for, a more convenient form is:

$$(1 + p)^n = 1 + np + \frac{n(n-1)}{2!} p^2 + \frac{n(n-1)(n-2)}{3!} p^3 + \ldots$$

or:

$$(a + b)^n = a^n + na^{n-1}b + \frac{n(n-1)}{2!} a^{n-2}b^2 + \ldots$$

To find the coefficient of x^4 in the expansion of $(2 - 3x)^{10}$, we would work out:

$$\binom{10}{4} 2^6 (-3x)^4 = 210 \times 64 \times 81x^4$$
$$= 1\,088\,640x^4,$$

so the coefficient is 1 088 640. You can see that we have to raise $(-3x)$ to the power of 4 to get a term in x^4. Then the term (2) has to be raised to the power $10 - 4 = 6$.

Be very careful when expanding in series like this that you remember to bracket the appropriate terms. In the last example, for instance, the term in x^4 is $\binom{10}{4} 2^6 (-3x)^4$ and not $\binom{10}{4} 2^6 \times -3x^4$.

Here are a couple of examples from exam papers:

Example	The first three terms in the expansion of $(1 + ax)^n$, in ascending powers of x, are:

$$1, 2x \text{ and } \frac{3}{2}x^2.$$

Determine the values of a and n.

Solution	Using the alternative form gives the first three terms of $(1 + ax)^n$ as:

$$1 + n(ax) + \frac{n(n-1)}{2}(ax)^2$$

We can then equate the coefficients of x and x^2 in both this and the given series for two equations in n and a.

x-coefficient: $na = 2$ ... ①

x^2-coefficient: $\dfrac{n(n-1)}{2}a^2 = \dfrac{3}{2}$ ... ②

From ① , $a = \dfrac{2}{n}$. Substituting this into ② ,

$$\frac{n(n-1)}{2} \times \left(\frac{2}{n}\right)^2 = \frac{3}{2}$$

$$\frac{n(n-1)}{2} \times \frac{4}{n^2} = \frac{3}{2} \quad \Rightarrow 2\frac{(n-1)}{n} = \frac{3}{2}$$

$$\Rightarrow 4(n-1) = 3n \Rightarrow 4n - 4 = 3n$$

$$\Rightarrow n = 4 \qquad \text{into ①}$$

$$\Rightarrow a = \frac{1}{2}$$

Here's another example where the first term in the bracket is not 1.

Example

The first three terms in the expansion of $(a - \frac{1}{3}x)^6$, in ascending powers of x, are $64 - 64x + bx^2$ where a and b are constants.

Find the value of a and the value of b.

Solution

Using the alternative form, $(a - \frac{1}{3}x)^6 = a^6 + 6 \times a^5 \left(-\frac{1}{3}x\right) + \frac{6(5)}{2} \times a^4 \left(-\frac{1}{3}x\right)^2$

$$= a^6 - 2a^5x + \frac{5a^4x^2}{3}$$

Equating constants, $a^6 = 64 \Rightarrow a = \pm 2$

From the x-coefficient, $-2a^5 = -64$, so a must be $+2$

The x^2-coefficient is then $\dfrac{5 \times 16}{3} = \dfrac{80}{3} = b$

The solution is then $a = 2$ and $b = \dfrac{80}{3}$.

You should now be able to answer Exercises 2 to 6 on p. 126.

Solving equations

We saw in the previous module how we can find an approximate value for a root of the equation $f(x) = 0$ by looking for a change in sign of the function $f(x)$. The next stage is to improve the accuracy of this root by successive approximations, getting closer (hopefully) to the actual value. The method of using the last value to estimate the next is called *iteration* or an *iterative procedure*, i.e. one which is repeated until the root is accurate to the required number of decimal places.

Suppose, for example, that we wanted to find the square root of 2. We could be given the interative procedure

$$x_{n+1} = \frac{x_n^2 + 2}{2x_n} \qquad [A]$$

and the starting point $x_0 = 1$. Putting $n = 0$ into [A] gives

$$x_1 = \frac{x_0^2 + 2}{2x_0}$$

and when $x_0 = 1$, $x_1 = \dfrac{1 + 2}{2} = 1.5$

We now use this value to calculate x_2.

$$x_2 = \frac{x_1^2 + 2}{2x_1} = \frac{1.5^2 + 2}{2 \times 1.5} = 1.417 \text{ (3 decimal places)}$$

Actually, the calculator display gives 1.416666667, so instead of adjusting this, we can put this into memory and find x_3:

$$x_3 = \frac{x_2^2 + 2}{2x_2} = 1.414215686$$

and the
$$x_4 = 1.414213562$$
$$x_5 = 1.414213562$$

This is already accurate to 9 decimal places – in this case the procedure is said to *converge* quickly.

Here's another example of this method.

Example   Show that the equation $x^3 - x - 2 = 0$ has a root between 1 and 2.

By using the iterative procedure $x_{n+1} = \sqrt[3]{x_n + 2}$ with $x_0 = 1.5$, find this root to 4 decimal places.

Solution   If we put $f(x) = x^3 - x - 2$

then $f(1) = -2$

and $f(2) = 4$

There is a change in sign in the function: so for some value of x in range $1 < x < 2$, $f(x) = 0$, i.e. has a root.

With $x_0 = 1.5$, $x_1 = \sqrt[3]{x_0 + 2} = \sqrt[3]{3.5} = 1.51829$ (working to an extra d.p.)
$x_2 = 1.52093$
$x_3 = 1.52131$
$x_4 = 1.52137$
$x_5 = 1.52138$

We can see that the sequence is converging to 1.5214 (4 d.p.).

You should now be able to answer Exercises 7 and 8 on p. 126.

EXERCISES

1 Find the coefficient of x^3 in $(1 + x)^7$

2 Find the terms in:

a x^3 in $(1 + 3x)^4$ **b** x^2 in $(1 + 7x)^5$ **c** x^4 in $(1 + \frac{x}{2})^6$

d x^5 in $(1 - 2x)^5$

Find the coefficient of:

e x^2 in $(1 - x)^7$ **f** x^4 in $(1 - \frac{x}{2})^5$

3 Find, in ascending powers of x, the first three terms in the expansions of:

a $(2 - x)^6$ **b** $(2 + x)(2 - x)^6$

4 Find the coefficient of a^3 in the expansion of $(2 + 3a)^5$.

5 Find, in ascending powers of x, the first three terms in the expansion of $(1 + ax)^6$.

Given that the first two non-zero terms in the expansion of

$(1 + bx)(1 + ax)^6$ are 1 and $\dfrac{-21x^2}{4}$, find the possible values of a and b.

6 Find the first three terms in the expansion of $(1 - 2x)^5$ in ascending powers of x, simplifying the coefficients.

Given that the first three terms in the expansion of $(a + bx)(1 - 2x)^5$ are $2 + cx + 10x^2$, state the value of a and hence find the value of b and c.

7 Show that the equation $x^3 - 5x + 1 = 0$ has a root between 2 and 3.

With a starting value of 2, use the iterative procedure $x_{n+1} = \sqrt[3]{5x_n - 1}$ to give this root correct to three places of decimals.

8 Show that the equation $x = -\ln(4 + x)$ has a root between -1.1 and -1. Use the iteration $x_{n+1} = -\ln(4 + x_n)$, starting with the value of -1, to find the value of this root correct to three decimal places.

SUMMARY

Both the topics in this section relate to approximations: the binomial expansion is an introduction to a method whereby a function can be expressed as a series in ascending powers of the variable rather as we can represent a fraction by a number to a certain number of decimal places. The other technique we have studied allows us to solve certain otherwise insoluble problems to as great an accuracy as we require.

SECTION

11

Probability and the mathematics of uncertainty

INTRODUCTION We have probably all encountered questionnaires of some kind or other, designed to extract information from us which can be used to improve service or sales. In this section we shall see how the information from surveys of this kind can be ordered, analysed and presented. We shall also deduce some important results in the theory of probability which will enable us to calculate the formal probability of certain particular events.

The target population and samples

When carrying out surveys, the group from which we hope to find information, the *target population*, is usually large. It would be extremely costly and time-consuming to attempt to collect data from each member. In many cases it would be impossible.

Instead, we think of taking only a fraction of the population, called a *sample*. We do this on the assumption that the sample is a reasonable representation of the whole – i.e. that the characteristics of the sample will be more or less those of the population.

Obviously we need to be careful here: all data is subject to a degree of variability – we could by chance select a group of items which are *not typical* of the population. They may be much higher than average or much lower. So before the sample is picked we have to make some decisions:

● How large a sample is necessary?

● Do we take a completely random sample?

● Do we need information from different groups within the population, e.g. members from each of several different age-groups?

The first necessity is some idea of the target population – it would be useful to have a complete list of all the possible members, called a *sample frame*, but in many cases this is only an ideal. From the knowledge that is available the sample is selected according to the various requirements: the size, for example, will depend on the degree of confidence we need to have that the sample will be a true reflection of the target population.

Once this has been done, and the method of eliciting the information has been established, the data is collected. This could be done by:

- someone asking questions
- an experimenter making measurements
- a member of the target population sending in their own completed questionnaires, etc.

Displaying data

Once the data has been collected – at this stage it is called *raw* data – it has to be ordered and presented before much sense can be made of it. The type of presentation will depend largely on the use that is to be made of the material. If only a general idea of the way the data is distributed is required, the most suitable presentation may be a visual display, using some kind of chart or graph. On the other hand, where precise information is needed the data might be better given in numerical form.

Discrete and continuous data

There is a distinction between two different types of data:

- discrete
- continuous.

Discrete data can only take a certain set of values (frequently whole numbers but not necessarily). Examples of discrete data would be the number of people entering a shop in a half-hour interval or the price of a cup of coffee. There is a large range of possible values for either of these, but within these ranges there are values which they cannot take: the number of people could not be $19\frac{1}{3}$, for instance, and neither, in ordinary circumstances, could the price of a cup of coffee be 53.7p.

Continuous data on the other hand involves some measurement and then within the range of possible values any value is possible, the only restriction being the accuracy of the measuring instrument. The time that I take to walk to the shops or the weight of the apple I buy there could both theoretically be measured as accurately as required. They are both examples of continuous data.

Frequency distributions

In order to analyse the results, the data is frequently collected into various classes according to size. It is then much easier to form some idea of the principal features of the distribution of the items and calculate any appropriate parameters. Such a presentation is called a *frequency distribution*.

Suppose, for example, that a traffic survey of the number of cars passing a certain point in one minute gave the following data:

2, 5, 0, 1, 1, 6, 3, 1, 4, 1, 5, 4, 3, 2, 1, 1, 1, 2, 5, 3, 2, 0, 1, 4, 2

The frequency of occurrence of each number can then be found and the results tabulated.

Table 11.1

Number of cars	0	1	2	3	4	5	6
Frequency	2	8	5	3	3	3	1

When there are a large number of values that the items can take, the data can be grouped so that in each class there may be a number of values, for example, 16–20, 21–25 etc. In fact, if the data is continuous, the frequency distribution has to be constructed like this.

Class limits and boundaries

The figures for the groups mentioned above, i.e. 16–20, 21–25, are called the *class limits*. If the variable, say X, is *discrete*, the items belonging to this particular class are just 16, 17, 18, 19 and 20: the *lower class boundary*, i.e. the least value of X that belongs to this class, is 16 and similarly the *upper class boundary* is 20.

If the variable X is continuous and has been rounded to the nearest integer, a value for X of 16 could be anything within the range $15.5 \leq X < 16.5$. In this case, the lower class boundary for the class 16–20 would be 15.5 and similarly the upper class boundary would be 20.5.

One exception for a continuous variable occurs when the variable X is the age of a person. Since a person has the same age up to the day before a birthday, the usual rules for rounding do not apply: X is 25 means that $25 \leq X < 26$.

Presentation

If there is no great concern for accuracy, an immediate impression of the main points of the data can be given visually. When the data has already been grouped into classes with their respective frequencies, the distribution can be shown on a chart with columns whose heights are proportional to the number of items in the class. Suppose, for example, that we had collected some data on the age of persons going on a particular type of holiday.

Table 11.2

Age	Number of people
0–19	54
20–39	94
40–59	33
60–79	15
80–99	4
100+	0

The corresponding chart would look like the one in Figure 11.1, with the limits for the rectangles being the class boundaries.

Figure 11.1

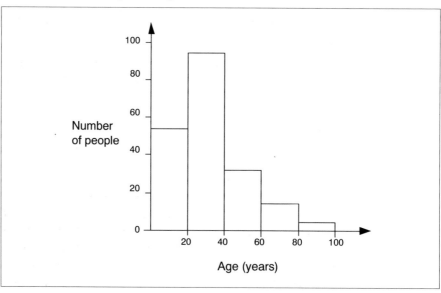

In this case all the classes had the same width, i.e. 20 years. If the widths are not equal, the height of each column has to be adjusted so that the *area is proportional to the frequency*. For example, if the class 20–39 had been divided for some reason into the two classes, 20–29 and 30–39 with corresponding frequencies 54 and 40, the height of these two columns would be doubled (to 108 and 80) to compensate for the fact that their bases are only half the standard width. The revised chart would look like:

Figure 11.2

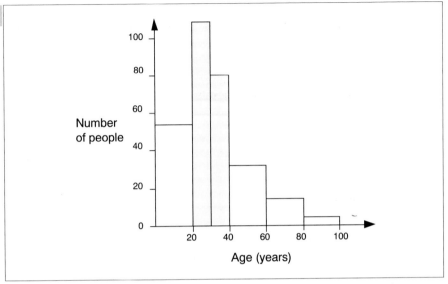

Similarly, if the width was double that of a standard class, the height would only be half of what it would otherwise have been. This type of chart is called a *histogram*.

Instead of the number of people within a certain age-group, we can also be interested in the number of people less than a certain age. Taking the same data as before, we can make another table:

Table 11.3

Age	<20	<40	<60	<80	<100
Number	54	148	181	196	200

where each entry is the sum of all the previous entries. We plot a series of points, the upper class boundaries (in this case 20, 40, etc.) being the horizontal variable and the cumulative frequency the vertical variable. When we join these points with straight lines, we have a *cumulative frequency polygon*.

Figure 11.3

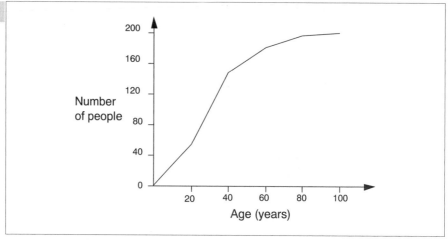

The next few sections will be concerned with finding estimates for the middle point of the data and the likely variation within the data. We shall see how the cumulative frequency polygon provides a basis for the quick calculation of certain of these qualities.

You should now be able to complete Exercises 1 and 2 on p. 144.

Mean

This is probably the most widely used estimate for the middle point of the data. The *mean* of a set of data is the arithmetic average, i.e. the sum of all the items divided by the number of items. When the data is given singly, e.g. 7, 4, 2, 6, 11 this is easily found:

$$\frac{7 + 4 + 2 + 6 + 11}{5} = \frac{30}{5} = 6$$

More usually the data is given in the form of a frequency distribution. With single values the method is essentially the same: find the sum of the items and the number of items and divide the sum by the number.

If we return to the data on the number of cars, which had the following frequency distribution table:

Table 11.4

Number of cars	0	1	2	3	4	5	6
Frequency	2	8	5	3	3	3	1

we can see that there are two 0's, eight 1's, etc., and so the sum of these is simply $2 \times 0 + 8 \times 1 + 5 \times 2 + 3 \times 3 + 3 \times 4 + 3 \times 5 + 1 \times 6 = 60$.

To find the number of items, we have to sum the frequencies,
i.e. 2 + 8 + 5 + 3 + 3 + 3 + 1 = 25. The average or mean of these data is then:

$$\frac{60}{25} = 2.4$$

If the items are collected into classes of numbers rather than single numbers, the mid-point of the class is taken to represent the class. Suppose we had a frequency distribution for the number of double-faults served per set by a particular tennis-player.

Table 11.5

Number double faults	4–6	7–9	10–12
Frequency	19	22	9

We take the mid-point of the class 4–6 to be 5, that of 7–9 to be 8 and that of 10–12 to be 11. This then gives the sum of the items as $19 \times 5 + 22 \times 8 + 9 \times 11 = 370$. Adding the frequencies gives $19 + 22 + 9 = 40$ and so the mean is:

$$\frac{370}{50} = 7.4$$

(Note that the mean can be a decimal even when the values in the distribution are whole numbers.) In this case, since we have no information about the precise number of the different items making up each class the mean is an *estimate*.

We can express the formula for the mean using the Σ-notation if we suppose that all the items in the data are labelled $x_1, x_2, x_3, \ldots x_n$ so that we can refer to a general item as x_i. Then Σx_i means the sum of all the items, and so the mean of these x's usually written $\bar{x}$, is given by:

$$\bar{x} = \frac{\Sigma x_i}{n}$$

For the case where the data is given in a frequency distribution, we can suppose that the frequency corresponding to the value x_i is f_i. The revised formula for the mean then looks like:

$$\bar{x} = \frac{\Sigma x_i f_i}{\Sigma f_i}$$

Median

The median is the value of the middle item of a distribution once they have been arranged in order of size. For example, given the data 7, 2, 11, 3, 6, we could first arrange it in ascending order, 2, 3, 6, 7, 11 and find that the middle item has a value of 6 which is the *median*. We might use the median in a situation where the mean would give an unrepresentative picture owing to the presence of some extreme items having an effect in excess of their significance.

If the data is presented as a frequency distribution we have first to find the position of the middle term. With three terms, the middle is the second term, 1 ②️ 3, i.e. in position 2. With four terms, the middle is between the second and third terms, 1 ②️–③️ 4, i.e. in position $2\frac{1}{2}$.

The formula for finding the median is 'add one onto the number of terms and divide by 2'. Having found the position, we then have to see which value occupies this place.

For example, in the distribution of the number of cars there are 25 items, so the middle term will be in position $\frac{1}{2}(25 + 1) = 13$. To find out where this term is, we total the number in the classes from the beginning. There are 2 items in the first class, so the 3rd item begins the second class. There are 10 items in the first two classes, so the 11th item starts the third class. Since there are five items in this class it will also contain the 13th item, and so the median value is 2.

Mode

The modal value or *mode* of a distribution is the most frequently occurring value (or values: there could be more than one mode). So in the frequency table for the number of cars we see that 1 is the most frequent value, occurring 8 times and so 1 is the mode.

Variance and standard deviation

We want to have some idea of how a typical item from a distribution is likely to deviate from the central point. Take the two sets of data 7, 6, 5 and 11, 2, 5. They have the same mean, 6, but the first set are clustered round this point whilst the items in the second set show more variability.
A convenient way of putting a value on the amount of deviation is to find the average of the squares of the distances of each point from the mean.

Figure 11.4

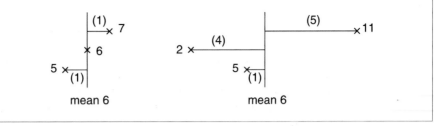

In the first set, the differences of the points from the mean are respectively 1, 0 and –1. Squaring these gives 1, 0 and 1, with an average of:

$$\frac{1 + 0 + 1}{3} = \frac{2}{3}$$

For the second set, the differences are 5, –4, –1 with corresponding squares of 25, 16 and 1. The average of these is:

$$\frac{25 + 16 + 1}{3} = \frac{42}{3} = 14$$

These two averages, $\frac{2}{3}$ and 14, are called the *variances* of the sets of data. If we take the square root of the variance we have a quantity called the *standard deviation* and this is the most commonly used measure of the variability of the data.

In symbols:

$$\text{Variance} = \frac{\Sigma(x_i - \bar{x})^2}{n}$$

where, as before x_i means a general item, and $\bar{x}$ is the mean of the data.

$$\text{Standard deviation} = \sqrt{\text{Variance}}$$

$$= \sqrt{\frac{\Sigma(x_i - \bar{x})^2}{n}}$$

In practice, it would be time-consuming to calculate the mean and then for each item find the difference and square. The alternative formula is more convenient, particularly as data is frequently presented in the form Σx_i and Σx_i^2. The formula is:

$$\text{Variance} = \frac{\Sigma x_i^2}{n} - \left(\frac{\Sigma x_i}{n}\right)^2 = \frac{\Sigma x_i^2}{n} - \bar{x}^2$$

with, of course, the standard deviation the square root of this. For the first set of data, $\Sigma x_i^2 = 49 + 36 + 25 = 110$. With $\bar{x} = 6$, the variance using the alternative formula works out as:

$$\frac{110}{3} - 6^2 = \frac{2}{3} \text{ as before.}$$

You can check that the formula also works for the second set.

When the data is given in the form of a frequency table, the formula for the variance is:

$$\text{Variance} = \frac{\Sigma f_i x_i^2}{\Sigma f_i} - \bar{x}^2$$

In the calculation of the variance and standard deviation, every item of the data plays a part. This can make for greater accuracy, but it also means that there is an increased sensitivity to untypical items in the distribution which may have a disproportionate effect on the estimate.

For example, the majority of a work-force may have a roughly similar wage while a small number of managers have a very much higher wage. If these higher wages are taken into account, the standard deviation can give a false picture of the typical deviation from the mean wage. In this case, alternative ways of expressing the spread of the data might be considered. We will look at these in the next section.

You should now be able to complete Exercises 3, 4, 5 and 6 on pp. 144–145.

Applications of the cumulative frequency polygon

One alternative way of giving an idea of the spread is to ignore a certain percentage of the lower and higher values. The most commonly used figure is 25% so that only the middle 50% of the distribution is considered. The difference between the lower and upper boundaries of this portion is called the *interquartile range*. It can be found quite easily from a cumulative frequency polygon by finding the values corresponding to cumulative frequencies of 25% and 75% and finding the difference between these values.

We can take the cumulative frequency polygon that we looked at previously as an example. There are 200 items, so we are looking for the values corresponding to the cumulative frequency of

$$\frac{25}{100} \times 200 \quad \text{and} \quad \frac{75}{100} \times 200 \quad \text{i.e. 50 and 150.}$$

Figure 11.5

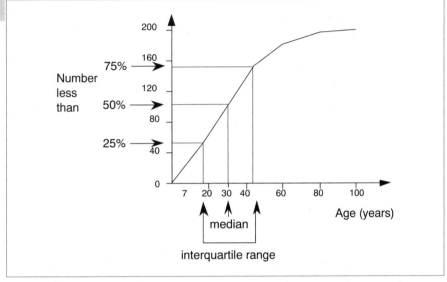

These are about 18 and 46 and so the interquartile range is estimated as 28 years.

From the same polygon we can also form an estimate of the *median* if we find the value corresponding to the $\frac{n}{2} = \frac{200}{2} = 100^{\text{th}}$ position. From the age scale, this is about 30 years.

Finally, mention can be made of a very quick way of expressing the variability of the data. It is the *range*, found simply by the difference between the lowest and highest values of the items in the data. However, except for giving a very rough idea it is of no great practical use since only two items, possibly very untypical, are taken into account with the distribution of the rest disregarded.

You should now be able to complete Exercise 7 on p. 146.

Probability

You are familiar with experiments which have several possible outcomes, for example an ordinary six-sided die is rolled with outcomes of 1, 2, 3, 4, 5 or 6 landing uppermost. In this situation the probability of any particular outcome, say obtaining a 6, is defined as follows:

$$\text{Probability} = \frac{\text{number of favourable outcomes}}{\text{number of possible outcomes}}$$

when the experiment is repeated a large number of times. In this particular case, the probability is easy to work out: since all the outcomes are equally likely, we expect the ratio of 6's to throws to be 1:6, i.e. the probability of obtaining a six on any throw is $\frac{1}{6}$.

Tree diagrams

Suppose we had a bag of 10 counters, 6 of which are yellow and 4 green. If a counter is picked at random, the probability of choosing a yellow counter is:

$$\frac{\text{number of yellow counters}}{\text{number of all counters}} = \frac{6}{10} = \frac{3}{5}$$

and similarly the probability of choosing a green counter is $\frac{4}{10} = \frac{2}{5}$

If this counter is replaced and another counter drawn, the probability that this second counter is yellow is the same as before, i.e. $\frac{3}{5}$.

If, however, the first counter is *not* replaced, there is a different situation depending on the colour of the first counter drawn. When the first counter drawn is yellow, there will be 9 counters remaining of which 5 are yellow and 4 green. In this case, the probability of the second counter being yellow is $\frac{5}{9}$ and being green is $\frac{4}{9}$. When the first counter drawn is green, of the 9 counters remaining 6 are yellow and only 3 green. The probabilities for the second counter are then $\frac{6}{9}$ for yellow and $\frac{3}{9}$ for green.

In order to present these different situations in a clear and systematic way, we make a *tree-diagram*. Here all the different outcomes for the experiment are listed and the appropriate probabilities, depending on previous outcomes, are put in half-way along each 'branch'. The experiment we have just been considering could be set out:

Figure 11.6

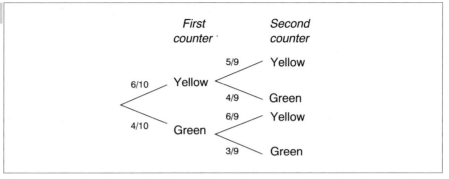

You can see that the probability of, for instance, a yellow for the second counter depends on which 'branch' is taken, i.e. whether the first counter was yellow or green.

To find probabilities from the tree diagram, we use a rule which is true for most of the time. The rule is *'and is ×, or is + '*. So, for example, to find the probability of a yellow *and* then a yellow, i.e. two yellows, we follow the double yellow branch which has probabilities:

$$\frac{6}{10} \times \frac{5}{9} = \frac{30}{90} = \frac{1}{3}$$

On the other hand, to find the probability of choosing different colours, we can follow *either* the yellow and green branch, i.e.: $\frac{6}{10} \times \frac{4}{9}$,

or the green and yellow branch, i.e. $\frac{4}{10} \times \frac{6}{9}$.

Since it is either or, we *add* these two products, giving a final probability of different colours as:

$$\frac{6}{10} \times \frac{4}{9} + \frac{4}{10} \times \frac{6}{9} = \frac{48}{90} = \frac{8}{15}$$

Combinations of events

We need to express some ideas more formally before we continue.

- A *trial* (or experiment) is something that is carried out, like rolling a die or tossing a coin.

- An *outcome* is the result of this trial, for example the die landing with a 5 uppermost.

- An *event* is a particular collection, or *set*, of these possible outcomes: rolling an odd number with the die for example, i.e. the set of outcomes { 1, 3, 5 }. These events can be labelled: the last set of outcomes could be called *A* and a different set { 3, 6 }, i.e. the set of multiples of 3 uppermost on the die, could be called *B*.

There are also some symbols which are used when talking about sets:

- $n(event)$ is the number of outcomes in an event, so that $n(A) = 3$ and $n(B) = 2$ for the events above.

- $A \cap B$ means the set of events that are in both the event A *and* the event B. With A the set $\{1, 3, 5\}$ and B the set $\{3, 6\}$ as above, $A \cap B = \{3\}$ since only the outcome 3 is in each of the events A and B.

- $A \cup B$ means the set of events that are in event A *or the* event B (or both). With A and B as above, $A \cup B = \{1, 3, 5, 6\}$

To find $n(A \cup B)$, i.e. the number of outcomes in A or B, we take all the outcomes in A with all the outcomes of B, giving the set $\{1, 3, 5, 3, 6\}$. This means that any outcomes in both A and B are counted twice, once for A and once for B, so from this set we subtract the outcomes in $A \cap B$ leaving the unduplicated set: $\{1, 3, 5, 6\}$

This gives

$$n(A \cup B) \quad = \quad n(A) \quad + \quad n(B) \quad - \quad n(A \cap B)$$

(in this case $\quad 4 \quad = \quad 3 \quad + \quad 2 \quad - \quad 1$)

Dividing throughout by n(possible outcomes) gives:

$$P(A \cup B) = P(A) + P(B) - P(A \cap B)$$

since we saw at the beginning of this section that the probability of any event X is $\dfrac{n(X)}{n(\text{possible})}$.

Here is an example of its use.

Example   The letters P, Q, R and S are arranged at random in a row. Find the probability that Q is the first letter or R is the last letter (or both).

Solution   In symbols, we want P(Q first $\cup$ R last) using the formula,

$$P(\text{Q first} \cup \text{R last}) = P(\text{Q first}) + P(\text{R last}) - P(\text{Q first} \cap \text{R last})$$

Now Q can be in any one of four positions, so $P(\text{Q first}) = \frac{1}{4}$ and similarly $P(\text{R last}) = \frac{1}{4}$. To find P(Q first $\cap$ R last) we start with Q being first.

This leaves 3 letters and so the probability of it being R that is last in this case will be $\frac{1}{3}$.

So overall, the probability of Q being first and R being last is $\frac{1}{4} \times \frac{1}{3} = \frac{1}{12}$

and $P(\text{Q first} \cup \text{R last}) = \frac{1}{4} + \frac{1}{4} - \frac{1}{12} = \frac{5}{12}$

Conditional probability

We'll take the experiment of rolling a six-sided die again and let A be the event 'the number showing is even' and let B be the event 'the number showing is a multiple of 3'. We have seen that since all the outcomes of the experiment are equally likely, the probability of A, i.e. $P(A)$, is:

$$\frac{n(A)}{n(\text{possible})} = \frac{3}{6} = \frac{1}{2}$$

Now suppose we are told that the event B has occurred. What is the probability *now* that A occurred at the same time? The number of possible outcomes has been narrowed to just the two in B, i.e. {3 and 6}. Of these possible outcomes there is only one which is also in event A, i.e. an even number as well as a multiple of 3.

So the probability of A occurring, given that B has occurred, written in short as $P(A\,|\,B)$, is $\frac{1}{2}$. This is actually the same as the probability of A occurring with no other information.

This is not always the case. If we took event C to be 'the number uppermost is a prime number', the outcomes in C are {2, 3, 5}. The conditional probability of A, given that C has occurred, i.e. $P(A\,|\,C)$, is found by seeing how many of the possible outcomes in C are also in A, i.e. how many outcomes are in $A \cap C$. This is just one, 3 being prime and also a multiple of 3, and so:

$$P(A\,|\,C) = \frac{n(A \cap C)}{n(C)} = \frac{1}{3}$$

In fact, if we divide the first fraction top and bottom by the number of total outcomes, we arrive at another important formula which is true for any events A and C:

$$P(A\,|\,C) = \frac{P(A \cap C)}{P(C)}$$

This can also be rearranged to:

$$P(A \cap C) = P(A\,|\,C)\,P(C)$$

Independent events

We say that two events A and B are *independent* if:

$$P(A \cap B) = P(A)P(B)$$

or equivalently

$$P(A|B) = P(A)$$

If we take the events A, B and C from the last section, we saw that $P(A) = \frac{1}{2}$, i.e. the fact that B had occurred had not affected the probability of A. These events A and B are then independent. On the other hand, with $P(A) = \frac{1}{2}$ still, we saw that $P(A|C) = \frac{1}{3} \neq P(A)$ and so C has affected A; the events are not independent.

Sometimes it is obvious that two events are independent: if I roll a die and then toss a coin I do not expect the outcome on the die to affect the outcome of the coin. At other times, as with the events A, B and C above, it is not obvious and the separate probabilities have to be calculated and compared before a conclusion can be reached.

Let's have a look now at some examples where these ideas are used.

Example   Events A and B are such that $P(A \cup B) = \frac{3}{4}$, $P(A) = \frac{2}{3}$ and $P(B) = \frac{1}{4}$. Find:

a $P(A \cap B)$ **b** $P(A|B)$ **c** $P(B|A)$

and state with a reason whether A and B are independent events.

Solution   **a** Using the formula $P(A \cup B) = P(A) + P(B) - P(A \cap B)$

we have $\frac{3}{4} = \frac{2}{3} + \frac{1}{4} - P(A \cap B)$

$\Rightarrow P(A \cap B) = \frac{2}{3} + \frac{1}{4} - \frac{3}{4} = \frac{1}{6}$

b $P(A|B) = \dfrac{P(A \cap B)}{P(B)} = \dfrac{\frac{1}{6}}{\frac{1}{4}} = \dfrac{2}{3}$

c $P(B|A) = \dfrac{P(B \cap A)}{P(A)} = \dfrac{\frac{1}{6}}{\frac{2}{3}} = \dfrac{1}{4}$

Since we have $(P(A|B) = \frac{2}{3} = P(A)$, $P(B|A) = \frac{1}{4} = P(B)$

and also $P(A)\,P(B) = \frac{2}{3} \times \frac{1}{4} = \frac{1}{6} = P(A \cap B)$. The events A and B are independent (any one of the three would be sufficient).

Example   A boy uses a home-made metal detector to look for valuable metallic objects on a beach. There is a fault in the machine which causes it to signal the presence of only 95% of the metallic objects over which it passes and to signal the presence of 6% of the non-metallic objects over which it passes. Of the objects over which the machine passes, 20% are metallic.

a   Find the probability that a given object over which the machine passes is metallic and the machine gives a signal.

b   Find the probability of a signal being received by the boy for any given object over which the machine passes.

c   Find the probability that the boy has found a metal object when he receives a signal.

Solution   A systematic way of answering this would be to make a tree-diagram, with the probabilities in percentages converted to decimals.

Figure 11.7

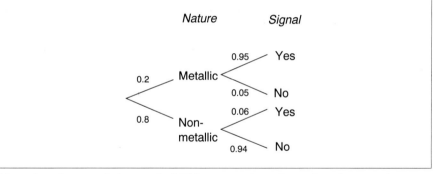

Note that the remaining probabilities are written in so that the sum for any particular choice is 1.

It is now easier to answer the questions

a   P(Metallic and Signal): we go along this branch and find this is
$0.2 \times 0.95 = 0.19$

b   P(Signal). There are two possible branches here, either Metallic and Signal or Non-Metallic and Signal. The total probability is the sum of these, i.e. $0.2 \times 0.95 + 0.8 \times 0.06 = 0.19 + 0.048 = 0.238$

c   This is the conditional probability P(Metallic | Signal), which is

$$\frac{\text{P(Metallic and Signal)}}{\text{P(Signal)}} = \frac{0.19 \ \ (\text{from } \mathbf{a})}{0.238 \ \ (\text{from } \mathbf{b})}$$

$$= 0.798 \ (3 \text{ d.p.})$$

You should now be able to complete Exercises 8, 9 and 10 on p. 146.

EXERCISES

1 A runner records her time for a circuit in her training programme. The times, to the nearest second, on 40 occasions are given below:

230	221	236	224	250	215	237	228	239	218
204	240	235	231	220	244	232	246	222	233
229	247	212	242	238	226	245	208	258	230
234	222	249	232	217	255	236	226	238	220

Construct a grouped frequency table with a class interval of 10, the first class being 200–209, and draw a histogram to display the data.

2 The table shows the masses, arranged in groups, of the members of a rowing club. The masses are measured tothe nearest kg.

Mass (kg)	60–69	70–74	75–79	80–89	90–109
No of members	3	12	25	22	18

Draw a histogram to illustrate these data. (Remember that the rectangles have as their horizontal limits the *class boundaries*. In this case, since the figures are rounded, these boundaries will be 59.5–69.5, 69.5–74.5, etc.)

3 The marks of 5 students in an examination were 29, 30, 51, 53, 57.

Calculate the mean mark and the standard deviation.

4 A group of 20 people played a game. The table below shows the frequency distribution of their scores.

Score	1	2	4	x
Number of people	2	5	7	6

Given that the mean score is 5, find:

a the value of x

b the variance of the distribution

5 The number of people, including the driver, on a certain late-night train service on a hundred separate occasions is given below:

5 6 1 4 9 7 5 6 7 4 3 2 3 5 5 5 9 8 5 8

8 2 7 5 3 3 4 7 8 5 9 4 6 6 4 7 3 2 5 6

4 7 5 6 8 6 3 5 4 3 8 6 5 2 9 7 4 3 7 2

3 2 8 4 6 5 2 8 8 1 5 4 6 3 4 2 6 5 5 8

6 7 5 9 1 3 4 5 6 7 9 7 4 5 1 6 3 9 4 4

a Produce a frequency table for these data.

b Hence, or otherwise, calculate estimates of the mean and the standard deviation of this population.

6 As a result of examining a sample of 700 invoices, a sales manager drew up the following grouped frequency table of sales, rounded to the nearest pound.

Amount on invoice (£)	Number of invoices
0–9	44
10–19	194
20–49	157
50–99	131
100–149	69
150–199	40
200–499	58
500–749	7

a Calculate estimates of the mean and the standard deviation of the population from which this sample was taken.

b Explain why the mean and the standard deviation might not be the best summary statistics to use with these data.

7 The masses at birth of 250 babies born in a certain hospital were recorded in kg to the nearest 0.1 kg. The table below shows the frequency distribution of these masses.

Mass (kg)	1.0–1.4	1.5–1.9	2.0–2.4	2.5–2.9	3.0–3.4	3.5–3.9	4.0–4.4
Frequency	2	6	17	60	95	60	10

a State the limits between which the masses of the babies in the group 2.5–2.9 must lie.

Construct the cumulative frequency table, and draw the cumulative frequency polygon.

Use this curve to estimate:

b the median

c the interpercentile range (i.e. the range of values between the lower 10% and upper 10%).

8 A number is chosen at random from the integers from 1 to 30 inclusive. Find the probability that the number chosen is:

a a multiple of either 3 or 11

b a multiple of either 3 or 5 or both.

9 A bag contains four white balls and five blue balls. If two balls are drawn at random one after the other, without replacement, calculate the probability that they are of the same colour.

10 Two players, A and B, play a match consisting of a series of games. The probability that A will win any one game is $\frac{3}{5}$, and games cannot be drawn. Games are played until either A or B has won 2 games. Calculate the probability:

a that the match is finished in 2 games,

b that A wins the match.

Given that A has won the match, calculate the probability:

c that only 2 games were played.

SUMMARY   You should now have a clearer idea of how data can be collected, ordered and presented so that important features can easily be seen or calculated and also have an idea of how the probability of certain events can be found.

Section 1

1 Multiply the bracket out:

$px^2 + 2pqx + pq^2 + r = 4x^2 - 6x + 5$

x^2-coeff: $p = 4$

x-coeff: $2pq = -6 \Rightarrow 8q = -6 \Rightarrow q = -\dfrac{3}{4}$

constant: $pq^2 + r \Rightarrow \dfrac{9}{4} + r = 5 \Rightarrow r = \dfrac{11}{4}$

2 Expanding the bracket:

$(a - c^2) - 2bcx - b^2x^2 = 2 - 4x - 4x^2$

x^2-coeff: $-b^2 = -4 \Rightarrow b^2 = 4$
$\Rightarrow b = 2$ (since positive)

x-coeff: $-2bc = -4 \Rightarrow -4c = -4 \Rightarrow c = 1$

constant: $a - c^2 = 2 \Rightarrow a - 1 = 2 \Rightarrow a = 3$ [2]

3 One way of solving this is simply to multiply the brackets on the left hand side to give

$mt^3 - 4mt^2 + 5mt + nt^2 - 4nt + 5n$

$= (m)t^3 + (n - 4m) t^2 + (5m - 4n) t + 5n$

Comparing this expansion with the given cubic,

$m = 2$ [1]
$n - 4m = p$ [2]
$5m - 4n = q$ [3]
$5n = 5$ [4]

From [4], $n = 1$: this and $m = 2$ gives $p = -7$, $q = 6$.

The values are 2, 1, −7 and 6, respectively.

4 **a** $\dfrac{x + 2}{2 - x}$ **b** $\dfrac{x^2 - y^2}{x^2 + y^2}$ **c** $x - 1$ **d** $\dfrac{1}{x}$

   e $\dfrac{1 - 3x}{1 - x^4}$ **f** $\dfrac{2(2x + 1)}{2x - 1}$

5 **a** Suppose:

$$\dfrac{2x + 10}{(x - 1)(x + 2)} \equiv \dfrac{A}{x - 1} + \dfrac{B}{x + 2}$$

$$= \dfrac{A(x + 2) + B(x - 1)}{(x - 1)(x + 2)}$$

Then we have to choose A and B so that:

$$2x + 10 \equiv A(x + 2) + B(x - 1)$$

$x = -2$: $6 = -3B \Rightarrow B = -2$

$x = 1$: $12 = 3A \Rightarrow A = 4$

So: $\dfrac{2x + 10}{(x - 1)(x + 2)} = \dfrac{4}{x - 1} - \dfrac{2}{x + 2}$

b Suppose:

$$\dfrac{7}{(1 - 2x)(4 - x)} = \dfrac{A}{1 - 2x} + \dfrac{B}{4 - x}$$

$$= \dfrac{A(4 - x) + B(1 - 2x)}{(1 - 2x)(4 - x)}$$

i.e. $7 = A(4 - x) + B(1 - 2x)$

$x = 4$: $7 = -7B \Rightarrow B = -1$

$x = \dfrac{1}{2}$: $7 = \dfrac{7}{2}A \Rightarrow A = 2$

So: $\dfrac{7}{(1 - 2x)(4 - x)} = \dfrac{2}{1 - 2x} - \dfrac{1}{4 - x}$

c $\dfrac{2x}{x^2 - 1} = \dfrac{2x}{(x - 1)(x + 1)} \equiv \dfrac{A}{x - 1} + \dfrac{B}{x + 1}$

$$= \dfrac{A(x + 1) + B(x - 1)}{(x - 1)(x + 1)}$$

i.e. $2x \equiv A(x + 1) + B(x - 1)$

$x = -1$: $-2 = -2B \Rightarrow B = 1$

$x = 1$: $2 = 2A \Rightarrow A = 1$

So: $\dfrac{2x}{x^2 - 1} = \dfrac{1}{x - 1} + \dfrac{1}{x + 1}$

6 **a** Let:

$$\dfrac{3x^2}{(x - 2)(x^2 + 2)} \equiv \dfrac{A}{x - 2} + \dfrac{Bx + C}{x^2 + 2}$$

$$= \dfrac{A(x^2 + 2) + (x - 2)(Bx + c)}{(x - 2)(x^2 + 2)}$$

i.e. $3x^2 \equiv A(x^2 + 2) + (x - 2)(Bx + C)$

$x = 2$: $12 = 6A$ $\Rightarrow$ $A = 2$

x^2-coeff: $3 = A + B$ $\Rightarrow$ $B = 1$

constant: $0 = 2A - 2C$ $\Rightarrow$ $C = 2$

i.e. $\dfrac{3x^2}{(x-2)(x^2+2)} = \dfrac{2}{x-2} + \dfrac{x+2}{x^2+2}$

b Let $\dfrac{x^2-2x+5}{(x-1)(x^2+1)} = \dfrac{A}{x-1} + \dfrac{Bx+C}{x^2+1}$

$= \dfrac{A(x^2+1) + (x-1)(Bx+C)}{(x-1)(x^2+1)}$

i.e. $x^2-2x+5 = A(x^2+1) + (x-1)(Bx+C)$

$x = 1:$ $4 = 2A$ $\Rightarrow$ $A = 2$

x^2-coeff: $1 = A + B$ $\Rightarrow$ $B = -1$

constant: $5 = A - C$ $\Rightarrow$ $C = -3$

i.e. $\dfrac{x^2-2x+5}{(x-1)(x^2+1)} = \dfrac{2}{x-1} - \dfrac{x+3}{x^2+1}$

c Let $\dfrac{8-3x}{(x+4)(x^2+4)} = \dfrac{A}{x+4} + \dfrac{Bx+C}{x^2+4}$

$= \dfrac{A(x^2+4) + (x+4)(Bx+C)}{(x+4)(x^2+4)}$

i.e. $8-3x = A(x^2+4) + (x+4)(Bx+C)$

$x = -4;$ $20 = 20A \Rightarrow A = 1$

x^2-coeff: $0 = A + B \Rightarrow B = -1$

constant: $8 = 4A + 4C \Rightarrow C = 1$

i.e. $\dfrac{8-3x}{(x+4)(x^2+4)} = \dfrac{1}{x+4} + \dfrac{1}{x^2+4}$

7 a Let $\dfrac{4+5x-x^2}{(x-1)(x+1)^2} \equiv$

$\dfrac{A}{x-1} + \dfrac{B}{x+1} + \dfrac{C}{(x+1)^2}$

$= \dfrac{A(x+1)^2 + B(x-1)(x+1) + C(x-1)}{(x-1)(x+1)^2}$

i.e. $4+5x-x^2 \equiv$
$A(x+1)^2 + B(x-1)(x+1) + C(x-1)$

$x = 1:$ $8 = 4A \Rightarrow A = 2$

$x = -1:$ $-2 = -2C \Rightarrow C = 1$

x^2-coeff: $-1 = A + B \Rightarrow B = -3$

i.e. $\dfrac{4+5x-x^2}{(x-1)(x+1)^2} = \dfrac{2}{x-1} - \dfrac{3}{x+1} + \dfrac{1}{(x+1)^2}$

b Let $\dfrac{4x^2-12x-15}{(x+2)(x-3)^2} \equiv$

$\dfrac{A}{x+2} + \dfrac{B}{x-3} + \dfrac{C}{(x-3)^2}$

$= \dfrac{A(x-3)^2 + B(x+2)(x-3) + C(x+2)}{(x+2)(x-3)^2}$

i.e. $4x^2-12x-15 =$
$A(x-3)^2 + B(x+2)(x-3) + C(x+2)$

$x = 3:$ $-15 = 5C$ $\Rightarrow C = -3$

$x = -2:$ $25 = 25A$ $\Rightarrow A = 1$

x^2-coeff: $4 = A + B$ $\Rightarrow B = 3$

i.e. $\dfrac{4x^2-12x-15}{(x+2)(x-3)^2} = \dfrac{1}{x+2} + \dfrac{3}{x-3} - \dfrac{3}{(x-3)^2}$

c Since the power on the top is the same as the power on the bottom, we have to divide first of all.

$\dfrac{x^2+1}{x^2+3x+2} = 1 - \dfrac{(2x+1)}{x^2+3x+2}$.

$\dfrac{2x+1}{(x+1)(x+2)} = \dfrac{A}{x+1} + \dfrac{B}{x+2}$

$= \dfrac{-1}{x+1} + \dfrac{3}{x+2}$

i.e. $\dfrac{x^2+1}{x^2+3x+2} = 1 + \dfrac{1}{x+1} - \dfrac{3}{x+2}$

8 a
$$\begin{array}{r} 2x-1 \\ x-3 \overline{\smash{)}\ 2x^2-7x-1} \\ 2x^2-6x \\ \hline -x-1 \\ -x+3 \\ \hline -4 \end{array}$$

Answer is $2x - 1 + \dfrac{-4}{x+3}$

b
$$\begin{array}{r} x^2-5x+6 \\ x-1 \overline{\smash{)}\ x^3-6x^2+11x-6} \\ x^3-x^2 \\ \hline -5x^2+11x \\ -5x^2+5x \\ \hline 6x-6 \\ 6x-6 \\ \hline \end{array}$$

Answer is $x^2 - 5x + 6$

c
$$\begin{array}{r} x^2-7x+12 \\ x+2 \overline{\smash{)}\ x^3-5x^2-2x+24} \\ x^3+2x^2 \\ \hline -7x^2-2x \\ -7x^2-14x \\ \hline 12x+24 \\ 12x+24 \\ \hline \end{array}$$

Answer is $x^2 - 7x + 12$

d

$$2x - 1 \overline{\smash{\big)}\ 6x^3 + 7x^2 - x - 2} \quad \overset{\displaystyle 3x^2 + 5x + 2}{}$$

$$\underline{6x^3 - 3x^2}$$
$$10x^2 - x$$
$$\underline{10x^2 - 5x}$$
$$4x - 2$$
$$\underline{4x - 2}$$

Answer is $3x^2 + 5x + 2$

9 26

10 -5

11 $(x - 1)\,(x - 3)\,(x + 3)$

12 $(x + 1)\,(x - 3)\,(x + 5)$

13 $(x - 2)\,(x^2 + 5x + 2)$

14 $a = 2, b = 3$ Only real root: $x = 2$

15 $h = 4, g = -1$ Remaining factors: $(x + 2), (x + 3)$

Section 2

1 **a** 2 **b** 3 **c** 2 **d** 1 **e** 4 **f** 5

2 **a** 5 **b** 10 **c** 30 **d** 21

3 **a** 1/2 **b** -1 **c** -2 **d** 2/3 **e** 5/2 **f** 4

4 **a** $3 \log 2$ **b** $-2 \log 2$

5 **a** $\log \left(\dfrac{x^3}{y^2} \right)$ **b** $\log (p^5 q)$

6 **a** $x = 16$ **b** $x = 1$

　　c $3^x = 2$ or $3^x = 3 \Rightarrow x = 0.63$ or 1 **d** $\dfrac{5}{3}$

7 **a** $x = 11.97$ **b** $y = 3.03$

8 $n = 66$ (2 significant figures)

9 $x = 1.82$

10 **a** $x = 7$ **b** $x = -5$

11 **a** $t = 1 \Rightarrow n = 6e^{0.3(0)} = 6e^0 = 6$

　　b $n = 49 \Rightarrow 49 = 6e^{0.3(t-1)}$

　　$\Rightarrow \dfrac{49}{6} = e^{0.3(t-1)}$

　　Taking ln's

　　$\ln \dfrac{49}{6} = \ln (e^{0.3(t-1)}) = 0.3\,(t - 1)$

　　$\Rightarrow\ t - 1 = \dfrac{1}{0.3} \ln \dfrac{49}{6}$

　　$\Rightarrow\ t = 1 + \dfrac{1}{0.3} \ln \dfrac{49}{6} = 8$ weeks (nearest week)

12 **a** When $t = 0$, $N = 10^{26}$

　　b A negative exponential curve has the shape

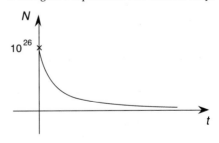

　　c When $N = 5 \times 10^{25}$ (NB not 10^{13})

　　$5 \times 10^{25} = 10^{26}\, e^{-2t}$

　　$\dfrac{5 \times 10^{25}}{10^{26}} = \dfrac{1}{2} = e^{-2t}$

　　Taking ln's

　　$-2t = \ln \dfrac{1}{2} \qquad \Rightarrow t = -\dfrac{1}{2} \ln \dfrac{1}{2}$

　　$\Rightarrow t = 0.35$ seconds (2 d.p.)

Section 3

1 a Directly: $y - 4 = 3(x - 3) \Rightarrow y = 3x - 5$

  b Has same gradient, $\frac{1}{2} \Rightarrow y - 4 = \frac{1}{2}(x - 2)$

   $\Rightarrow 2y = x + 6$

  c Given line has gradient $-\frac{3}{2}$, so required

   gradient is $\frac{2}{3}$ and required equation

   $y + 3 = \frac{2}{3}(x + 1) \Rightarrow 3y = 2x - 7$

  d Gradient is $\frac{6}{3}$ i.e. 2. Using first, $y - 3 = 2(x - 1)$

   $\Rightarrow y = 2x + 1$

2 Taking averages, point has coordinates

  $\left(\dfrac{7 + 3}{2}, \dfrac{-1 + (-5)}{2}\right)$ i.e. $(5 - 3)$

3 a Gradient of line between A and B

   is $\dfrac{-2}{6} = -\dfrac{1}{3}$

   $\Rightarrow$ Gradient of line perpendicular to this is 3.
   Passes through the mid-point of AB,

   $\left(\dfrac{1 + 7}{2}, \dfrac{7 + 5}{2}\right)$, i.e. $(4, 6)$

   Equation is then $y - 6 = 3\,(x - 4) \Rightarrow y = 3x - 6$

  b Gradient BC is $\dfrac{5 + 2}{7} = 1$, through $(0, -2)$,

   then equation is $y + 2 = x$ i.e. $y = x - 2$.
   Solving equations simultaneously,

   $3x - 6 = x - 2$

   $\Rightarrow 2x = 4 \Rightarrow x = 2, y = 0$

   i.e. the point is $(2, 0)$.

4 If the variables are connected by the
  relationship $y = ax^b$, we can take logs of both
  sides to give:

  $\begin{aligned} \log_e y &= \log_e (ax^b) \\ &= \log_e a + \log_e(x^b) \\ &= \log_e a + b \log_e x \end{aligned}$

  Now if we make the new variables $\log_e y$ and
  $\log_e x$, calling these Y and X respectively, we
  would expect these to be of the form

  $y = bX + C$ where $C = \log_e a$, a constant

  which is a straight line, gradient b, intercept C.

The table below shows these new variables.

x	12	15	22	28	35
y	75.9	54.3	30.6	21.3	15.3
$\log_e x\ (= X)$	2.48	2.71	3.09	3.33	3.56
$\log_e y\ (= Y)$	4.33	3.99	3.42	3.06	2.73

Your graph should look like this.

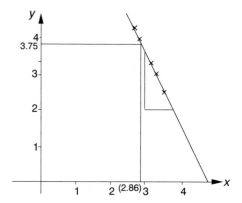

The points lie very nearly on a straight line, so
we are justified in our assumption that the
relationship is of the form $y = ax^b$.

a For b, we want the gradient. Using two
suitable points,

  $b = \dfrac{\text{difference}}{\text{difference}}$

   $= \dfrac{1.96 - 3.54}{4 - 3} = -1.6$ (to one d.p.)

To find a, we'll use the fact that we now know
the relationship between X and Y to be

  $Y = -1.6X + C$ [1]

and from the graph, when $Y = 0$, $X = 5.24$.
Putting this into [1] gives

  $0 = (-1.6)(5.24) + C$

  $\Rightarrow C = 8.38$

  But $C = \log_e a$

  so $a = e^{8.38} = {,}359$

   $= 4{,}400$ (to two significant figures)

b When $y = 42.5$, $Y = 3.75$

  From the graph at this point $X = 2.89$,

  so $x = e^{2.89} = 18.1$ (to three s.f.)

5 **a** $Y = y^2$ $\quad X = x$

b $Y = \dfrac{1}{y}$ $\quad X = \dfrac{1}{x}$

c Divide by $x \Rightarrow \dfrac{y^2}{x} = ax + b$

Put $Y = \dfrac{y^2}{x} \, X = x$

d Divide by $x \Rightarrow y = a + \dfrac{by}{x}$

Put $Y = y \, X = \dfrac{y}{x}$

or Divide by $y \Rightarrow x = a\dfrac{x}{y} + b$

Put $Y = x \, X = \dfrac{x}{y}$

6 **a** Taking lns of both sides,

$$\ln y \quad = \ln\left(\dfrac{x^a}{b}\right)$$

$$= \ln(x^a) - \ln b$$

$$= a \ln x - \ln b$$

Then putting $Y = \ln y$. $X = \ln x$ gives the required form

$$Y \quad = aX - \ln b$$

b lns of both sides again,

$$\ln(e^y) = \ln(ab^x)$$

$$y \quad = \ln a + \ln b^x$$

$$= \ln a + x \ln b$$

So we don't need to change the variables.

c lns again,

$$\ln y \quad = \ln(x^b e^a)$$

$$= \ln x^b + \ln e^a$$

$$= b \ln x + a$$

So we need to put $Y = \ln y$ and $X = \ln x$.

Section 4

1 **a** Using $1 + \tan^2\theta = \sec^2\theta$,

$$1 + \tan^2\theta = \dfrac{4}{3}$$

$$\tan^2\theta = \dfrac{4}{3} - 1 = \dfrac{1}{3}$$

$$\tan\theta = \pm\dfrac{1}{\sqrt{3}}$$

b $1 + \tan^2\theta = \sec^2\theta \Rightarrow 1 + 1 = \sec^2\theta$

$$\sec^2\theta = 2$$

$$\sec\theta = \pm\sqrt{2}$$

c Using $1 + \cot^2\theta = \operatorname{cosec}^2\theta$

$$1 + \cot^2\theta = 4$$

$$\cot^2\theta = 3$$

$$\cot\theta = \pm\sqrt{3}$$

d $1 + \cot^2\theta = \operatorname{cosec}^2\theta \Rightarrow 1 + 3 = \operatorname{cosec}^2\theta$

$$\operatorname{cosec}^2\theta = 4$$

$$\operatorname{cosec}\theta = \pm 2$$

2 From the triangles:

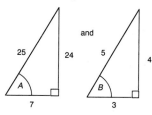

and

a $\cos A = \dfrac{7}{25}$ and $\tan A = \dfrac{24}{7}$

b $\sin B = \dfrac{4}{5}$ and $\tan B = \dfrac{4}{3}$

c $\sin(A + B) = \sin A \cos B + \sin B \cos A$

$$= \dfrac{24}{25} \times \dfrac{3}{5} + \dfrac{4}{5} \times \dfrac{7}{25}$$

$$= \dfrac{72 + 28}{125} = \dfrac{100}{125} = \dfrac{4}{5}$$

sin is positive in the second quadrant, so adding the angle A has pushed B to a symmetrical position in the second quadrant

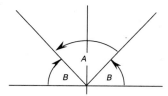

d $\cos(A+B)=\cos A\cos B-\sin A\sin B$

$$=\frac{3}{5}\times\frac{7}{25}-\frac{4}{5}\times\frac{24}{25}$$

$$=\frac{21-96}{125}=\frac{-75}{125}=\frac{-3}{5}$$

Same as $\cos B$, but negative since cos is
negative in the second quadrant.

e $\tan(A+B)=\dfrac{\tan A+\tan B}{1-\tan A\tan B}=\dfrac{\dfrac{24}{7}+\dfrac{4}{3}}{1-\dfrac{24}{7}\times\dfrac{4}{3}}$

$$=\frac{72+28}{21-96}=\frac{100}{-75}=-\frac{4}{3}$$

f $\tan(A-B)=\dfrac{\tan A-\tan B}{1+\tan A\tan B}=\dfrac{\dfrac{24}{7}-\dfrac{4}{3}}{1+\dfrac{24}{7}\times\dfrac{4}{3}}$

$$=\frac{72-28}{21+96}=\frac{44}{117}$$

3 $2[\sin\theta\cos60°-\cos\theta\sin60°]=$
$\qquad\qquad\cos\theta\cos60°-\sin\theta\sin60°$

$$2\left(\frac{1}{2}\sin\theta-\frac{\sqrt3}{2}\cos\theta\right)$$

$$=\frac{1}{2}\cos\theta-\frac{\sqrt3}{2}\sin\theta$$

$$\sin\theta-\sqrt3\cos\theta=\frac{1}{2}\cos\theta-\frac{\sqrt3}{2}\sin\theta$$

$$\left(\frac{2+\sqrt3}{2}\right)\sin\theta=\left(\frac{2\sqrt3+1}{2}\right)\cos\theta$$

$$\Rightarrow\frac{\sin\theta}{\cos\theta}=\frac{\frac{2\sqrt3+1}{2}}{\frac{2+\sqrt3}{2}}=\frac{2\sqrt3+1}{2+\sqrt3}\times\frac{2-\sqrt3}{2-\sqrt3}$$

i.e $\tan\theta=\dfrac{4\sqrt3-6+2-\sqrt3}{4-3}=3\sqrt3-4$

4   **a** $\cos\theta=\dfrac{4}{5}$, so triangle is

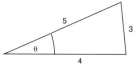

and $\sin\theta=\dfrac{3}{5}$, $\tan\theta=\dfrac{3}{4}$

$\cos2\theta\quad=2\cos^2\theta-1$

$$=2\left(\frac{16}{25}\right)-1=\frac{7}{25}$$

$$\tan2\theta=\frac{2\tan\theta}{1-\tan^2\theta}$$

$$=\frac{\dfrac{6}{4}}{1-\dfrac{9}{16}}=\frac{24}{16-9}=\frac{24}{7}$$

b $\tan\theta=\dfrac{4}{3}$

so $\cos\theta=\dfrac{3}{5}$, $\sin\theta=\dfrac{4}{5}$

$\cos2\theta=\cos^2\theta-\sin^2\theta$

$$=\frac{9}{25}-\frac{16}{25}=\frac{-7}{25}$$

(because bigger than 90°, hence
in second quadrant)

$$\tan2\theta=\frac{2\tan\theta}{1-\tan^2\theta}$$

$$=\frac{\dfrac{8}{3}}{1-\dfrac{16}{9}}=\frac{24}{9-16}=-\frac{24}{7}\;\text{(same reason)}$$

c $\sin\theta=\dfrac{7}{25}$

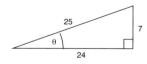

$$\cos\theta=\frac{24}{25},\ \tan\theta=\frac{7}{24}$$

$\cos2\theta=\cos^2\theta-\sin^2\theta$

$$=\frac{576}{625}-\frac{49}{625}=\frac{527}{625}$$

$$\tan2\theta=\frac{2\tan\theta}{1-\tan^2\theta}$$

$$=\frac{\dfrac{7}{12}}{1-\dfrac{49}{576}}=\frac{336}{576-49}=\frac{336}{527}$$

5 **a** $\dfrac{1 - \cos 2\theta}{\sin 2\theta} = \dfrac{2 \sin^2 \theta}{2 \sin \theta \cos \theta} = \dfrac{\sin \theta}{\cos \theta} = \tan \theta$

b $\cos 3\theta = \cos(2\theta + \theta)$

$= \cos 2\theta \cos \theta - \sin 2\theta \sin \theta$

$= (2 \cos^2 \theta - 1) \cos \theta - (2 \sin \theta \cos \theta) \sin \theta$

$= (2 \cos^2 \theta - 1) \cos \theta - 2 \sin^2 \theta \cos \theta$

$= (2 \cos^2 \theta - 1) \cos \theta - 2(1 - \cos^2 \theta) \cos \theta$

$= 2 \cos^3 \theta - \cos \theta - 2 \cos \theta + 2 \cos^3 \theta$

$= 4 \cos^3 \theta - 3 \cos \theta$

c $\dfrac{2 \tan \theta}{1 + \tan^2 \theta} = \dfrac{\dfrac{2 \sin \theta}{\cos \theta}}{1 + \dfrac{\sin^2 \theta}{\cos^2 \theta}}.$

Multiply through by $\cos^2 \theta$

$= \dfrac{\dfrac{2 \sin \theta \cos^2 \theta}{\cos \theta}}{\cos^2 \theta + \sin^2 \theta} = \dfrac{2 \sin \theta \cos \theta}{\cos^2 \theta + \sin^2 \theta}$

$= 2 \sin \theta \cos \theta \quad (\cos^2 + \sin^2 \theta = 1)$

$= \sin 2\theta$

d $\dfrac{1 + \cos \theta}{\sin \theta} = \dfrac{1 + (2 \cos^2 \frac{\theta}{2} - 1)}{2 \sin \frac{\theta}{2} \cos \frac{\theta}{2}}$

$= \dfrac{2 \cos^2 \frac{\theta}{2}}{2 \sin \frac{\theta}{2} \cos \frac{\theta}{2}}$

$= \dfrac{\cos \frac{\theta}{2}}{\sin \frac{\theta}{2}} = \cot \dfrac{\theta}{2}$

6 The linear function is $\sin x$, so we change $\cos 2x$ into a form containing only $\sin x$, i.e.

$\cos 2x = 1 - 2 \sin^2 x$

The equation then becomes:

$4(1 - 2 \sin^2 x) + 2 \sin x = 3$

i.e. $4 - 8 \sin^2 x + 2 \sin x = 3$

$8 \sin^2 x - 2 \sin x - 1 = 0$

$(4 \sin x + 1)(2 \sin x - 1) = 0$

$\sin x = -\dfrac{1}{4}$ or $\sin x = \dfrac{1}{2}$

a $x = 194.5°$ or $345.5°$

b $x = 30°$ or $150°$

i.e. $x = 30°, 150°, 194.5°$ or $345.5°$
(to one decimal place)

7 $2(1 - \cos^2 \theta) + 5 \cos \theta + 1 = 0$

$2 - 2 \cos^2 \theta + 5 \cos \theta + 1 = 0$

$2 \cos^2 \theta - 5 \cos \theta - 3 = 0$

$(2 \cos \theta + 1)(\cos \theta - 3) = 0$

So $\cos \theta = -\dfrac{1}{2}$ ($\cos \theta = 3$ has no solutions)

and $\theta = 120°$ or $240°$

8 $1 + \tan^2 \theta = 3 \tan \theta - 1$

$\tan^2 \theta - 3 \tan \theta + 2 = 0$

$(\tan \theta - 1)(\tan \theta - 2) = 0$

$\tan \theta = 1 \Rightarrow \theta = \dfrac{\pi}{4}$ or $-\dfrac{3\pi}{4}$

$\tan \theta = 2 \Rightarrow \theta = 1.11$ or -2.03

(put your calculator in radians for this one)

9 $(\text{cosec}^2 \theta - 1) + \text{cosec } \theta = 5$

$\text{cosec}^2 \theta + \text{cosec } \theta - 6 = 0$

$(\text{cosec } \theta + 3)(\text{cosec } \theta - 2) = 0$

$\text{cosec } \theta = -3 \Rightarrow \dfrac{1}{\sin \theta} = -3 \quad \Rightarrow \sin \theta = -\dfrac{1}{3}$

$\Rightarrow \theta = -19.5°$

or $-160.5°$

$\text{cosec } \theta = 2 \Rightarrow \dfrac{1}{\sin \theta} = 2 \quad \Rightarrow \sin \theta = \dfrac{1}{2}$

$\Rightarrow \theta = 30°$ or $150°$

Section 5

1 a $\dfrac{dy}{dx} = 6x^2 - 6 = 18$ when $x = 2$

b $\dfrac{dy}{dx} = e^x = 4.48$ when $x = 1.5$

c $\dfrac{dy}{dx} = \cos x = \dfrac{1}{2}$ when $x = \dfrac{\pi}{3}$

d $\dfrac{dy}{dx} = \sec^2 x = \dfrac{4}{3}$ when $x = \dfrac{\pi}{6}$

2 a $\dfrac{dy}{dx} = -x^3 \sin x + 3x^2 \cos x$

b $\dfrac{dy}{dx} = e^x (\sin x + \cos x)$

c $\dfrac{dy}{dx} = e^x (x^3 + 3x^2)$

d $\dfrac{dy}{dx} = x \times \dfrac{1}{x} + 1 \times \ln x = 1 + \ln x$

3 a $\dfrac{dy}{dx} = \dfrac{(x+1) \times 1 - x.1}{(x+1)^2} = \dfrac{x + 1 - x}{(x+1)^2}$

$= \dfrac{1}{(x+1)^2}$

b $\dfrac{dy}{dx} = \dfrac{(1-x^2) \times 2x - x^2 (-2x)}{(1-x^2)^2}$

$= \dfrac{2x - 2x^3 + 2x^3}{(1-x^2)^2} = \dfrac{2x}{(1-x^2)^2}$

c $\dfrac{dy}{dx} = \dfrac{(1+x)(-1) - (1-x) \times 1}{(1+x)^2}$

$= \dfrac{-1 - x - 1 + x}{(1+x)^2} = \dfrac{-2}{(1+x)^2}$

d $\dfrac{dy}{dx} = \dfrac{x^3 \times e^x - e^x \times 3x^2}{x^6} = \dfrac{e^x (x-3)}{x^4}$

e $\dfrac{dy}{dx} = \dfrac{x \times \frac{1}{x} - \ln x \times 1}{x^2} = \dfrac{1 - \ln x}{x^2}$

4 a $6x - 6x \dfrac{dy}{dx} - 6y + 4y \dfrac{dy}{dx} = 0$

$\Rightarrow \dfrac{dy}{dx} = \dfrac{6y - 6x}{4y - 6x} = \dfrac{3y - 3x}{2y - 3x}$

b $e^x \dfrac{dy}{dx} + e^x y - e^y - e^y x \dfrac{dy}{dx} = 0$

$\Rightarrow \dfrac{dy}{dx} = \dfrac{e^y - e^x y}{e^x - e^y x}$

c $\dfrac{-1}{x^2} - \dfrac{1}{y^2} \dfrac{dy}{dx} = e^y \dfrac{dy}{dx}$

$\Rightarrow \dfrac{dy}{dx} = \dfrac{-\frac{1}{x^2}}{e^y + \frac{1}{y^2}} = \dfrac{-y^2}{x^2 y^2 e^y + x^2}$

5 a $y = u^4$ where $u = 1 + 3x$ so $\dfrac{du}{dx} = 3$

$\dfrac{dy}{dx} = \dfrac{dy}{du} \times \dfrac{du}{dx} = 4u^3 \times 3 = 12u^3 = 12(1 + 3x)^3$

b $y = e^u$ where $u = x^2 \Rightarrow \dfrac{du}{dx} = 2x$

$\dfrac{dy}{dx} = \dfrac{dy}{du} \times \dfrac{du}{dx} = e^u \times 2x = 2xe^u = 2xe^{x^2}$

c $y = \tan u$ where $u = x^2 - 1 \Rightarrow \dfrac{du}{dx} = 2x$

$\dfrac{dy}{dx} = \dfrac{dy}{du} \times \dfrac{du}{dx} = \sec^2 u \times 2x = 2x \sec^2 (x^2 - 1)$

d $y = \cos u$ where $u = e^x \Rightarrow \dfrac{du}{dx} = e^x$

$\dfrac{dy}{dx} = \dfrac{dy}{du} \times \dfrac{du}{dx} = -\sin u \times e^x = -e^x \sin (e^x)$

6 a $3e^{3x}$ **b** $-e^{-x}$ **c** $-\sin x e^{\cos x}$

d $(1 - 3x^2) e^{x - x^3}$ **e** $\dfrac{1}{x} e^{\ln x} (= 1)$ **f** $5^x \ln 5$

7 a $-12x^3 (1 - x^4)^2$

b $\dfrac{1}{2} (4 - x^2)^{-1/2} \times -2x = \dfrac{-x}{\sqrt{4 - x^2}}$

c $4 \cos x (1 + \sin x)^3$

d $-2xe^{4 - x^2}$ **e** $\sin x e^{1 - \cos x}$ **f** $\dfrac{5}{1 + 5x}$

g $\dfrac{-2x}{4 - x^2}$ **h** $-8x \cos (1 - 4x^2)$

i $2e^x \cos (3 + 2e^x)$ **j** $-3x^2 \sin (x^3)$ **k** $\sin \left(\dfrac{\pi}{4} - x \right)$

l $3 \sec^2 (3x + 2)$ **m** $\dfrac{-1}{x} \sec^2 (3 - \ln x)$

8 $y = \dfrac{2x + 10}{(x-3)(x+1)} = \dfrac{A}{x-3} + \dfrac{B}{x+1} =$

$\dfrac{A(x+1) + B(x-3)}{(x-3)(x+1)}$

Then $2x + 10 \equiv A(x+1) + B(x-3)$

$x = -1 \quad 8 = -4B \Rightarrow B = -2$

$x = 3 \quad 16 = 4A \Rightarrow A = 4$

$y = \dfrac{4}{x-3} - \dfrac{2}{x+1} = 4(x-3)^{-1} - 2(x+1)^{-1}$

$\dfrac{dy}{dx} = -4(x-3)^{-2} + 2(x+1)^{-2};$

$\dfrac{d^2y}{dx^2} = 8(x-3)^{-3} - 4(x+1)^{-3}$

$$\frac{d^3y}{dx^3} = -24(x-3)^{-4} + 12(x+1)^{-4} =$$

$$\frac{-24}{(-1)^4} + \frac{12}{(3)^4} = -23\frac{23}{27}$$

9 **a** If $y = x^3 + x + 1$

$$\frac{dy}{dx} = 3x^2 + 1 = 4 \text{ when } x = 1$$

This is gradient of tangent therefore the gradient of the normal is $\frac{-1}{4}$

When $x = 1$, $y = 3$

Tangent: $y - 3 = 4\,(x - 1)$

i.e. $y = 4x - 1$

Normal: $y - 3 = \frac{-1}{4}\,(x - 1)$

$$y - 3 = \frac{1}{4} - \frac{1}{4}x$$

i.e. $y = 3\frac{1}{4} - \frac{1}{4}x$

b If $y = x + \sin x$

$$\frac{dy}{dx} = 1 + \cos x$$

When $x = \frac{\pi}{4}$

$$y = \frac{\pi}{4} + \frac{1}{\sqrt{2}} = \frac{4 + \pi\sqrt{2}}{4\sqrt{2}}$$

and $\frac{dy}{dx} = 1 + \frac{1}{\sqrt{2}}$ (= gradient of a tangent)

$$= \frac{\sqrt{2} + 1}{\sqrt{2}}$$

So gradient of normal $= \frac{-\sqrt{2}}{\sqrt{2} + 1}$

Tangent: $y - \left(\dfrac{\pi\sqrt{2} + 4}{4\sqrt{2}}\right) = \left(\dfrac{1 + \sqrt{2}}{\sqrt{2}}\right)\left(x - \dfrac{\pi}{4}\right)$

$$y = \left(\frac{1 + \sqrt{2}}{\sqrt{2}}\right)x + \frac{\pi\sqrt{2} + 4 - \pi - \pi\sqrt{2}}{4\sqrt{2}}$$

$$y = \left(\frac{1 + \sqrt{2}}{\sqrt{2}}\right)x + \frac{4 - \pi}{4\sqrt{2}}$$

Normal: $y - \left(\dfrac{\pi\sqrt{2} + 4}{4\sqrt{2}}\right) = \left(\dfrac{-\sqrt{2}}{\sqrt{2} + 1}\right)\left(x - \dfrac{\pi}{4}\right)$

$$y = \frac{(\pi\sqrt{2} + 4)\,(\sqrt{2} + 1) + \pi\sqrt{2}\,\sqrt{2}}{4\sqrt{2}\,(\sqrt{2} + 1)} - \left(\frac{\sqrt{2}}{\sqrt{2} + 1}\right)x$$

$$y = \frac{2\sqrt{2}\pi + 4 + \pi + 2\sqrt{2}}{4\,(\sqrt{2} + 1)} - \left(\frac{\sqrt{2}}{\sqrt{2} + 1}\right)x$$

10 Differentiating with respect to x,

$$6xy^3 + 9x^2y^2\frac{dy}{dx} - 3x^2y^2 - 2x^3y\frac{dy}{dx} = 4$$

Putting in (2, 1)

$$12 + 36\frac{dy}{dx} - 12 - 16\frac{dy}{dx} = 4$$

$$20\frac{dy}{dx} = 4 \Rightarrow \frac{dy}{dx} = \frac{1}{5}$$

Equation of tangent: $y - 1 = \dfrac{1}{5}(x - 2)$

$$\Rightarrow 5y - 5 = x - 2$$

$$5y = x + 3$$

Equation of normal: $y - 1 = -5\,(x - 2)$

$$\Rightarrow y - 1 = -5x + 10$$

$$y + 5x = 11$$

Section 6

1 a $\dfrac{e^{2x}}{2} + C$ **b** $\dfrac{-1}{3}\cos 3x + C$

c $\dfrac{1}{4}\sin 4x + C$ **d** $\dfrac{-1}{18}(1 - 3x)^6 + C$

2 $\displaystyle\int x \sin 3x \, dx = \dfrac{-x}{3}\cos 3x - \int \dfrac{-1}{3}\cos 3x \, dx$

$$= \dfrac{-x}{3}\cos 3x + \int \dfrac{1}{3}\cos 3x \, dx$$

$$= \dfrac{-x}{3}\cos 3x + \dfrac{1}{9}\sin 3x + C.$$

3 $\displaystyle\int_0^1 x \, e^{2x} \, dx = \dfrac{xe^{2x}}{2} - \int_0^1 \dfrac{e^{2x}}{2} \, dx$

$$= \left[\dfrac{xe^{2x}}{2} - \dfrac{e^{2x}}{4}\right]_0^1 = \dfrac{1}{4}(e^2 + 1).$$

4 a $\displaystyle\int x^2 \ln x \, dx = \int \ln x \, x^2 \, dx$

$$= \ln x \dfrac{x^3}{3} - \int \dfrac{x^3}{3}\dfrac{1}{x} \, dx$$

$$= \dfrac{x^3}{3}\ln x - \int \dfrac{x^2}{3} \, dx. \text{ (Always simplify)}$$

$$= \dfrac{x^3}{3}\ln x - \dfrac{x^3}{9} + C$$

b $\displaystyle\int x^2 \sin x \, dx$ $\quad u = x^2 \quad v' = \sin x$

$$u' = 2x \quad v = -\cos x$$

$$= -x^2 \cos x + 2\int x \cos x$$

$$u = x \quad v' = \cos x$$
$$u' = 1 \quad v = \sin x$$

$$= -x^2 \cos x + x \sin x - \int \sin x$$

$$= -x^2 \cos x + x \sin x + \cos x + C$$

5 $\displaystyle\int \ln x \, dx = \int \ln x \times 1 \, dx$

$$= \ln x \, x - \int x \dfrac{1}{x} \, dx$$

$$= x \ln x - \int 1 \, dx \text{ (Always simplify)}$$

$$= x \ln x - x + C.$$

6 In partial fractions,

$$\dfrac{1}{(1 + x)(2 - x)} = \dfrac{1}{3}\dfrac{1}{(1 + x)} + \dfrac{1}{3}\dfrac{1}{2 - x}$$

Then integral becomes

$\dfrac{1}{3}\displaystyle\int \left(\dfrac{1}{1 + x} + \dfrac{1}{2 - x}\right) dx$

$$= \dfrac{1}{3}\left[\ln(1 + x) - \ln(2 - x)\right] + C$$

$$= \dfrac{1}{3}\ln\left(\dfrac{1 + x}{2 - x}\right) + C$$

7 $\displaystyle\int_2^4 \dfrac{1}{2x^2 + x} \, dx = \int_2^4 \dfrac{1}{x(2x + 1)} \, dx$

$$= \int_2^4 \left[\dfrac{1}{x} - \dfrac{2}{2x + 1}\right] dx$$

$$= \left[\ln x - \ln(2x + 1)\right]_2^4$$

$$= \left[\ln\left(\dfrac{x}{2x + 1}\right)\right]_2^4$$

$$= \ln\dfrac{4}{9} - \ln\dfrac{2}{5} = \ln\dfrac{10}{9}$$

8 Let $f(x) = \dfrac{11x^2 + 4x + 12}{(2x + 1)(x^2 + 4)} = \dfrac{A}{2x + 1} + \dfrac{Bx + C}{x^2 + 4}$

$$= \dfrac{A(x^2 + 4) + (Bx + C)(2x + 1)}{(2x + 1)(x^2 + 4)}$$

Then $11x^2 + 4x + 12 = A(x^2 + 4) + (Bx + C)(2x + 1)$

Put $x = -\dfrac{1}{2} : \dfrac{51}{4} = \dfrac{17A}{4} \Rightarrow A = 3$

x^2-coefficient: $11 = A + 2B \Rightarrow B = 4$

Constant : $12 = 4A + C \Rightarrow C = 0$

i.e. $\displaystyle\int_0^4 f(x) \, dx = \int_0^4 \left(\dfrac{3}{2x + 1} + \dfrac{4x}{x^2 + 4}\right) dx$

$$= \left[\dfrac{3}{2}\ln(2x + 1) + 2\ln(x^2 + 4)\right]_0^4$$

$$= \left(\dfrac{3}{2}\ln 9 + 2\ln 20\right) - (2\ln 4)$$

$$= \dfrac{3}{2}\ln 9 + 2\ln 5$$

$$= \ln 27 + \ln 25 = \ln 675$$

9 a $\ln |x^2 + x + 1| + C$

b $\displaystyle\int \tan x \, dx = \int \dfrac{\sin x}{\cos x} \, dx$

$$= -\ln |\cos x| + C$$

$$= \ln |\sec x| + C$$

10 Put $u = 1 - x^2 \Rightarrow \dfrac{du}{dx} = -2x$, so $dx = \dfrac{du}{-2x}$

Integral becomes: $\displaystyle\int x\sqrt{1-x^2}\,dx = \int x\sqrt{u}\,\dfrac{du}{-2x}$

$\quad = -\dfrac{1}{2}\displaystyle\int \sqrt{u}\,du \qquad = -\dfrac{1}{2}\int u^{1/2}\,du$

$\quad = -\dfrac{1}{3}u^{3/2} + C \qquad = -\dfrac{1}{3}\left(1-x^2\right)^{3/2} + C$

11 Put $u = 1 + 4x^3 \Rightarrow \dfrac{du}{dx} = 12x^2$, so $dx = \dfrac{du}{12x^2}$

$\displaystyle\int \dfrac{x^2}{(1+4x^3)^2}\,dx = \int \dfrac{x^2}{u^2}$

$\dfrac{du}{12x^2} = \displaystyle\int \dfrac{1}{12}\,u^{-2}\,du = \dfrac{-1}{12}\,u^{-1} + C$

$\quad = \dfrac{-1}{12(1+4x^3)} + C$

12 $x = 7 \Rightarrow u = 9$; $x = 2 \Rightarrow u = 4$

Put $u = x + 2 \Rightarrow du = dx$. $x = u - 2$

$\displaystyle\int_2^7 \dfrac{4x}{\sqrt{x+2}}\,dx = \int_4^9 \dfrac{4(u-2)}{\sqrt{u}}\,du = \int_4^9 \left(\dfrac{4u}{\sqrt{u}} - \dfrac{8}{\sqrt{u}}\right)du$

$\quad = \displaystyle\int_4^9 \left(4u^{1/2} - 8u^{-1/2}\right)du$

$\quad = \left[\dfrac{8u^{3/2}}{3} - 16u^{1/2}\right]_4^9$

$\quad = (72 - 48) - \left(\dfrac{64}{3} - 32\right) = \dfrac{104}{3}$

13 $x = e^2 \Rightarrow u = 2$

$x = e \Rightarrow u = 1$

Put $u = \ln x$, then $du = \dfrac{dx}{x}$

$\displaystyle\int_e^{e^2} \dfrac{1}{x \ln x}\,dx = \int_1^{e^2} \dfrac{1}{\ln x}\,\dfrac{dx}{x}$

$\quad = \displaystyle\int_1^2 \dfrac{1}{u}\,du = \Big[\ln u\Big]_1^2 = \ln 2$

14 Using the formula gives:

$\displaystyle\int \sin^2 3x\,dx = \int \dfrac{1}{2}(1 - \cos 6x)\,dx$

$\quad = \dfrac{1}{2}\displaystyle\int (1 - \cos 6x)\,dx$

$\quad = \dfrac{1}{2}\left[x - \dfrac{\sin 6x}{6}\right] + C$

15 a $\displaystyle\int_0^2 x^4\,dx = \left[\dfrac{x^5}{5}\right]_0^2 = \dfrac{32}{5} - 0 = \dfrac{32}{5}$

b $\displaystyle\int_{-1}^0 (x^3 - x)\,dx = \left[\dfrac{x^4}{4} - \dfrac{x^2}{2}\right]_{-1}^0 = 0 - \left(\dfrac{1}{4} - \dfrac{1}{2}\right) = \dfrac{1}{4}$

c $\displaystyle\int_0^{\pi/2} \sin x\,dx = \Big[-\cos x\Big]_0^{\pi/2}$

$\quad = \left(\cos \dfrac{\pi}{2}\right) - (-\cos 0) = 0 - (-1) = 1$

d $\displaystyle\int_0^1 e^{-x}\,dx = \Big[-e^{-x}\Big]_0^1 = -e^{-1} - (-1) = 1 - \dfrac{1}{e}$

e $\displaystyle\int_1^3 \dfrac{1}{1+x}\,dx = \Big[\ln(1+x)\Big]_1^3$

$\quad = \ln 4 - \ln 2 = \ln \dfrac{4}{2} = \ln 2$

16 The area is $\displaystyle\int_1^2 \dfrac{x}{x^2+1}\,dx = \left[\dfrac{1}{2}\ln(x^2+1)\right]_1^2$

$\quad = \dfrac{1}{2}(\ln 5 - \ln 2) = \dfrac{1}{2}\ln\dfrac{5}{2}$

17 The shaded area is the difference between the areas under the two curves, $y^2 = 3x\ (\Rightarrow y = \sqrt{3x})$ and $y = \dfrac{1}{3}x^2$,

i.e. $\displaystyle\int_0^3 \sqrt{3x}\,dx - \int_0^3 \dfrac{1}{3}x^2$

$\quad \dot= \sqrt{3}\displaystyle\int_0^3 x^{\frac{1}{2}}\,dx - \int_0^3 \dfrac{1}{3}x^2$

$\quad = \sqrt{3}\left[\dfrac{2}{3}x^{\frac{3}{2}}\right]_0^3 - \left[\dfrac{1}{9}x^3\right]_0^3$

$\quad = 6 - 3 = 3 \text{ units}^2$

18 Gradient of chord $= \dfrac{15-3}{0--2} = \dfrac{12}{2} = 6$

$\dfrac{y-15}{x-0} = 6$

$y - 15 = 6x$

$y = 6x + 15$: equation of chord

a P = area enclosed by curve and chord AB

Q = area enclosed by curve, $y = 0$, $x = 0$ and $x = -2$

R = area enclosed by chord AB, $y = 0$, $x = 0$ and $x = -2$

$P = Q - R$

$Q = \displaystyle\int_{-2}^0 (15 - 3x^2)\,dx$

$\quad = \Big[15x - x^3\Big]_{-2}^0$

$\quad = (0-0) - (-30 + 8) = 22$

$R = \dfrac{1}{2} \times 2 \times (3 + 15) = 18$

$P = Q - R = 22 - 18 = 4$

b

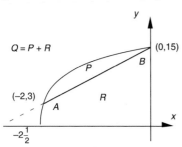

$Q = P + R$ (0,15)

B

P

(−2,3)

R

A

$-2\frac{1}{2}$

A rotation of R around x-axis produces volume V

A rotation of Q around x-axis produces volume W

Volume V is given by:

$$V = \frac{1}{3} \times \pi \times 15^2 \times 2\frac{1}{2} - \frac{1}{3} \times \pi \times 3^2 \times \frac{1}{2}$$

(using the difference between two cones)

$$= 186\,\pi$$

Volume W is given by:

$$W = \pi \int_{-2}^{0} y^2 \, dx$$

$$= \pi \int_{-2}^{0} (15 - 3x^2)^2 \, dx$$

$$= \pi \int_{-2}^{0} (225 - 90x^2 + 9x^4) \, dx$$

$$= \pi \left[225x - 30x^3 + \frac{9}{5}x^5 \right]_{-2}^{0}$$

$$= \pi\,(0) - \pi\left(-450 + 240 - \frac{288}{5}\right)$$

$$= \frac{1338\pi}{5}$$

The volume we want is the difference between these two volumes. And so:

$$W - V = \frac{1338}{5}\pi - 186\,\pi = \frac{408}{5}\pi$$

19 a R is rotated about the y-axis

Volume of solid generated, V

$$= \pi \int_{2}^{0} x^2 \, dy$$

$$= \pi \int_{2}^{0} (y^2 + 1)^2 \, dy$$

$$= \pi \int_{2}^{0} (y^4 + 2y^2 + 1) \, dy$$

$$= \pi \left[\frac{1}{5}y^5 + \frac{2}{3}y^3 + y \right]_{0}^{2}$$

$$= \pi \left(\left(\frac{32}{5} + \frac{16}{3} + 2 \right) - (0) \right)$$

$$= \frac{206}{15}\pi = 13\frac{11}{15}\pi$$

b R is rotated about the x-axis generating a volume V

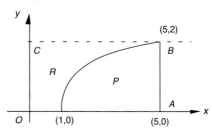

C (5,2) B

R P

A

O (1,0)   (5,0)

We find the value of V by calculating the volume that would be generated by rotating area P around the x-axis (we will call this W) and subtracting this from the volume generated from a rotation of rectangle $OABC$ around the x-axis.

$$W = \pi \int_{0}^{5} (x - 1) \, dx$$

$$= \pi \left[\frac{1}{2}x^2 - x \right]_{1}^{5}$$

$$= \pi \left(\left(\frac{25}{2} - 5 \right) - \left(\frac{1}{2} - 1 \right) \right)$$

$$= 8\,\pi$$

Volume caused by the rotation of $OABC$
$$= V + W = \pi\, r^2 \times h = \pi 4 \times 5 = 20\pi$$
$$V + W = 20\pi$$
$$V = 12\pi$$

20 The area of the first rectangle is width × height

$$= \frac{1}{5} \times \left(\frac{1}{5} \right)^2$$

the next is $\dfrac{1}{5} \times \left(\dfrac{2}{5} \right)^2$

then $\dfrac{1}{5} \times \left(\dfrac{3}{5} \right)^2$ and $\dfrac{1}{5} \times \left(\dfrac{4}{5} \right)^2$

Adding these gives $\dfrac{1}{5^3} (1^2 + 2^2 + 3^2 + 4^2)$

i.e. $\dfrac{1}{5^3} \left(\displaystyle\sum_{r=1}^{4} r^2 \right)$

Section 7

1 **a** Yes $\quad \dfrac{dy}{y} = 4x\,dx$

b Yes $\quad \cos y\,dy = \sin x\,dx$

c Yes $\quad \dfrac{y}{x}\dfrac{dy}{dx} = -4 \Rightarrow y\,dy = -4x\,dx$

d No

e Yes $\quad x\dfrac{dy}{dx} = 2y^2 - y \Rightarrow \dfrac{dy}{2y^2 - y} = \dfrac{dx}{x}$

f Yes $\quad y\dfrac{dy}{dx} = x - xy^2 = x(1 - y^2)$

i.e. $\dfrac{y\,dy}{1 - y^2} = x\,dx$

g No **h** No

i Yes $\quad y\dfrac{dy}{dx} = 2^x \times 2^{-y} \Rightarrow y2^y\,dy = 2^x\,dx$

j No

2 $\displaystyle\int\dfrac{dy}{y^2} = \int e^{-2x}\,dx$

$\dfrac{-1}{y} = \dfrac{-e^{-2x}}{2} + C$

When $x = 0$, $y = 1$, $-1 = -\dfrac{1}{2} + C \Rightarrow -\dfrac{1}{2} = C$

$-\dfrac{1}{y} = -\dfrac{e^{-2x}}{2} - \dfrac{1}{2} \Rightarrow \dfrac{1}{y} = \dfrac{1}{2}(e^{-2x} + 1)$

and $y = \dfrac{2}{1 + e^{-2x}}$

3 $\displaystyle\int\dfrac{dy}{y^2} = \int -x^{1/4}\,dx$

$-\dfrac{1}{y} = \dfrac{-4x^{5/4}}{5} + C$

When $x = 0$, $y = \dfrac{5}{2}$, $\dfrac{-2}{5} = 0 + C \Rightarrow C = -\dfrac{2}{5}$

$-\dfrac{1}{y} = \dfrac{-4x^{5/4}}{5} - \dfrac{2}{5}$

$-\dfrac{1}{y} = -\dfrac{2}{5}(2x^{5/4} + 1)$

When $x = 16$, $x^{5/4} = 32$

$\dfrac{1}{y} = \dfrac{2}{5}(65) = 26 \Rightarrow y = \dfrac{1}{26}$

4 $\displaystyle\int\dfrac{dy}{y} = \int -\dfrac{dx}{x^2}$

$\ln y = \dfrac{1}{x} + C$

If $x = 1$, $y = e \Rightarrow \ln e = 1 + C$

$1 = 1 + C$

$C = 0$

$\ln y = \dfrac{1}{x}$

$y = e^{1/x}$

5 **a** $2xy - x - 2y + 1 = 2xy + 6y + x + 3$

$8y = -2x - 2$

$y = -\dfrac{1}{4}(x + 1)$

b $y + ye^x = ye^{-x} + e^{-x}$

$y + ye^x - ye^{-x} = e^{-x}$

$y(1 + e^x - e^{-x}) = e^{-x}$

$y = \dfrac{e^{-x}}{1 + e^x - e^{-x}} = \left(\dfrac{1}{e^{2x} + e^x - 1}\right)$

6 $\dfrac{dN}{dt} = kN$

Rearranging $\displaystyle\int\dfrac{dN}{N} = \int k\,dt$

$\Rightarrow \ln N = kt + C \qquad [1]$

$t = 0$, $N = 1500 \Rightarrow \ln 1500 = C$

$\Rightarrow \ln N = kt + \ln 1500 \qquad [2]$

$t = 20$, $N = 3000 \Rightarrow \ln 3000 = 20k + \ln 1500$

$k = \dfrac{1}{20}(\ln 3000 - \ln 1500)$

$= \dfrac{1}{20}\left(\ln\dfrac{3000}{1500}\right) = \dfrac{1}{20}\ln 2$

$\Rightarrow \ln N = \left(\dfrac{1}{20}\ln 2\right)t + \ln 1500 \quad [3]$

$t = 80 \Rightarrow \ln N = 80 \times \dfrac{1}{20}\ln 2 + \ln 1500$

$= 4\ln 2 + \ln 1500$

$= \ln 2^4 + \ln 1500$

$= \ln 16 + \ln 1500$

$= \ln 16(1500)$

$= \ln 24000$

$\Rightarrow N = 24{,}000$

$N = 2000 \Rightarrow \ln 2000 = \left(\dfrac{1}{20}\ln 2\right)t + \ln 1500$

Rearranging:

$$\left(\frac{1}{20}\ln 2\right)t = \ln 2000 - \ln 1500$$

$$= \ln\frac{2000}{1500} = \ln\frac{4}{3}$$

$$\Rightarrow t = \frac{20\ln\frac{4}{3}}{\ln 2} = 8.3 \text{ hours}$$

But we're given that $t = 20$ hours

when $N = 3000$

∴ Time is difference between these, $20 - 8.3$

$= 11.7$ hours

$= 11$ hours 42 minutes.

7 $\dfrac{dh}{dt} = -kh$ [1]

Rearranging: $\displaystyle\int\frac{dh}{h} = -k\int dt$

$\Rightarrow \ln h = -kt + C$ [2] But $h = H$ when $t = 0$
(i.e. initially)

$\Rightarrow \ln H = C$

substituting in [2], $\ln h = -kt + \ln H$
Rearranging

$\Rightarrow -kt = \ln h - \ln H$

i.e. $-kt = \ln\dfrac{h}{H}$

Given that $h = \dfrac{H}{2}$ when $t = 3$

$$-3k = \ln\frac{\frac{H}{2}}{H} = \ln\frac{1}{2} = -\ln 2 \Rightarrow k = \frac{1}{3}\ln 2$$

when $h = \dfrac{H}{10}$, $\left(-\dfrac{1}{3}\ln 2\right)t = \ln\dfrac{\frac{H}{10}}{H} = \ln\dfrac{1}{10}$

$= -\ln 10$

$\Rightarrow t = \dfrac{\ln 10}{\frac{1}{3}\ln 2} = 10$ mins (nearest minute)

Section 8

1   Putting $x = 0$ gives $t = \dfrac{1}{2}$ and then

$$y = \left(\frac{1}{2}\right)^2 + 1 = \frac{5}{4}.$$

Putting $y = 0$ gives $t^2 + 1 = 0$, no solutions so the curve never crosses the x-axis. If we look at the equation defining y, we see that y can in fact never be less than 1, since $t^2 \geq 0$ for all values of t. y increases quicker than x. At the point, $t = 0$, $x = -1$. Taking a couple more points, say at $t = 1$ when $x = 1$, $y = 2$; $t = 3$ when $x = 5$, $y = 10$; $t = -1$ when $x = -3$, $y = 2$ and $t = -3$ when $x = -7$, $y = 10$, we can sketch the curve

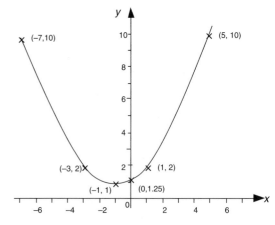

2   **a**   Rearranging the x-equation gives $t = x - 1$ and putting this into the y-equation gives

$$y = (x - 1) - 1 = x - 2$$

   b   From the x-equation, $t = \dfrac{x+1}{2}$, so

$$y = \left(\frac{x+1}{2}\right)^2 + 1$$

$$4y = x^2 + 2x + 5$$

   c   From the x-equation, $t = \dfrac{x}{2}$ and

$$y = \frac{1}{\frac{x}{2}} = \frac{2}{x}$$

3   **a**   Squaring, $x^2 = \cos^2 t$ and $y^2 = \sin^2 t$

Using $\cos^2 t + \sin^2 t = 1$,

$$x^2 + y^2 = 1$$

   b   Rearranging first of all, $\cos t = x + 1$ and $\sin t = y - 3$

Squaring these,

$\cos^2 t = (x + 1)^2$ and $\sin^2 t = (y - 3)^2$

and so　$(x + 1)^2 + (y - 3)^2 = 1$

c　Rearranging, $\cos t = \dfrac{x - 2}{3}$, $\sin t = \dfrac{y - 1}{3}$

and so　$\left(\dfrac{x - 2}{3}\right)^2 + \left(\dfrac{y - 1}{3}\right)^2 = 1$

$(x - 2)^2 + (y - 1)^2 = 9$

d　We use the relation $1 + \tan^2 t = \sec^2 t$

i.e. $1 + (x - 1)^2 = (1 - y)^2$

e　Squaring gives

$x^2 = (e^t + e^{-t})^2 = e^{2t} + 2 + e^{-2t}$

$y^2 = (e^t - e^{-t})^2 = e^{2t} - 2 + e^{-2t}$

Subtracting these, $x^2 - y^2 = 4$

4　Find $\dfrac{dy}{dt}$ and $\dfrac{dx}{dt}$ first of all

$\dfrac{dy}{dt} = 2t + 1$ and $\dfrac{dx}{dt} = 2t$

$\dfrac{dy}{dx} = \dfrac{\frac{dy}{dt}}{\frac{dx}{dt}} = \dfrac{2t + 1}{2t} = \dfrac{3}{2}$　when $t = 1$

Also, when $t = 1$, $x = 2$ and $y = 2$, and the tangent passes through this point.

Then the equation of the tangent is

$y - 2 \quad = \dfrac{3}{2}(x - 2)$

i.e. $2y - 4 \quad = 3x - 6$

$2y = 3x - 2$

5　$\dfrac{dy}{dt} = \dfrac{(1 - 2t)\, 2 - (1 + 2t)\, (-2)}{(1 - 2t)^2}$

$= \dfrac{2 - 4t + 2 + 4t}{(1 - 2t)^2} = \dfrac{4}{(1 - 2t)^2}$

$\dfrac{dx}{dt} = \dfrac{(1 - t)\, 1 - (1 + t)\, (-1)}{(1 - t)^2}$

$= \dfrac{1 - t + 1 + t}{(1 - t)^2} = \dfrac{2}{(1 - t)^2}$

$\dfrac{dy}{dx} = \dfrac{\frac{4}{(1 - 2t)^2}}{\frac{2}{(1 - t)^2}} = \dfrac{\frac{4}{1}}{\frac{2}{1}} = 2$ when $t = 0$

This is the gradient of the tangent – the gradient of the normal will be $\dfrac{-1}{2}$.

At the point where $t = 0$, $x = 1$, and $y = 1$. Then the normal has equation

$y - 1 = -\dfrac{1}{2}(x - 1) \Rightarrow 2y - 2 = -x + 1$

or　　　$2y + x = 3$

6　$\dfrac{dx}{dt} = -\sin t$；$\dfrac{dy}{dt} = -\sin t + \cos t$

$\dfrac{\frac{dy}{dt}}{\frac{dx}{dt}} = \dfrac{-\sin t + \cos t}{-\sin t}$

$= \dfrac{-\sin t}{-\sin t} + \dfrac{\cos t}{-\sin t}$

$= 1 - \cot t$

7　$\dfrac{dx}{dt} = 1 + \cos t$；$\dfrac{dy}{dt} = \sin t$

$\dfrac{dy}{dx} = \dfrac{\sin t}{1 + \cos t} = \dfrac{1}{1 + 0} = 1$　when $t = \dfrac{\pi}{2}$

When $t = \dfrac{\pi}{2}$, $x = \dfrac{\pi}{2} + 1$, $y = 1 - 0 = 1$

Equation of tangent is

$y - 1 = 1\left(x - \left[\dfrac{\pi}{2} + 1\right]\right)$

$y - 1 = x - \dfrac{\pi}{2} - 1$

$y = x - \dfrac{\pi}{2}$

This crosses the x-axis at point where $y = 0$, then $x = \dfrac{\pi}{2}$

P has co-ordinates $(\dfrac{\pi}{2}, 0)$.

Crosses the y-axis when $x = 0$, then $y = \dfrac{-\pi}{2}$.

Q has co-ordinates $(0, \dfrac{-\pi}{2})$.

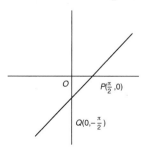

Area $\triangle POQ$ is $\frac{1}{2}$ base × height

$$= \frac{1}{2} \times \frac{\pi}{2} \times \frac{\pi}{2} = \frac{\pi^2}{8}$$

8 We'll make a rough sketch first of all – it belongs to the family of rectangular hyperbolas.

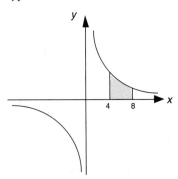

The formula for the area is $\int_{x_1}^{x_2} y \, dx$

we are substituting $y = \frac{4}{t}$ and using $x = 4t$ to find the limits and dx.

when $x = 8$, $4t = 8 \Rightarrow t = 2$

$x = 4$, $4t = 4 \Rightarrow t = 1$

$x = 4t \Rightarrow \dfrac{dx}{dt} = 4 \Rightarrow dx = 4dt$

the integral becomes

$$\int_1^2 \left(\frac{4}{t}\right) 4dt = 16 \int_1^2 \frac{1}{t} dt$$

$$= 16 \left[\ln t\right]_1^2$$

$$= 16 \left[\ln 2 - \ln 1\right]$$

$$= 16 \ln 2, \text{ the required area}$$

Section 9

1 a Using the sine rule,

$$\frac{a}{\sin A} = \frac{b}{\sin B}$$

i.e. $\dfrac{a}{\sin 40°} = \dfrac{12}{\sin 70°}$

$a = \dfrac{12 \times \sin 40°}{\sin 70°} = 8.2$ cm (to one decimal place)

b Find $\angle C$, which is $180° - 38° - 72° = 70°$.

Then $\dfrac{c}{\sin C} = \dfrac{a}{\sin A}$

i.e.

$a = \dfrac{15 \times \sin 38°}{\sin 70°} = 9.8$ cm (to one decimal place)

2 a $\dfrac{a}{\sin A} = \dfrac{b}{\sin B} \Rightarrow \dfrac{11}{\sin A} = \dfrac{10}{\sin 50°}$

$\sin A = \dfrac{11 \times \sin 50°}{10} = 0.84$

i.e. $\angle A = 57.4°$ or $122.6°$

the second solution is just possible – it gives

$\angle C = 180° - 50° - 122.6° = 7.4°$

b $\dfrac{2}{\sin A} = \dfrac{5}{\sin 40°} \Rightarrow \sin A = \dfrac{2 \sin 40°}{5} = 0.26$

i.e. $\angle A = 14.9°$ or $165.1°$

The second solution is not possible – we would be over $180°$ just by adding this value and $\angle B = 40°$.

3 a $\cos A = \dfrac{b^2 + c^2 - a^2}{2bc} = \dfrac{64 + 49 - 81}{112} = \dfrac{32}{112}$

i.e. $A = 73.4°$ (to one decimal place)

b $\cos A = \dfrac{3^2 + 2^2 - 4^2}{12} = \dfrac{-3}{12}$

i.e. $A = 104.5°$

4 a $a^2 = b^2 + c^2 - 2bc \cos A$

$\Rightarrow a^2 = 4 + 25 - 20 \cos 21.5°$

$= 29 - 18.61 = 10.39$

i.e. $a = 3.2$

b $a^2 = 4^2 + 5^2 - 40 \cos 115°$

$= 41 - 40 \, (-0.423) = 57.90$

i.e. $a = 7.6$

5 Call all the sides $2a$ for convenience.

a Move CD parallel to itself until it becomes BA. We want $B\hat{A}E$, so we take the triangle BAE:

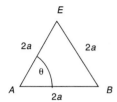

Since this is equilateral, θ, the required angle, is $60°$.

b Drop a perpendicular from E onto the base at N, say, and join AN

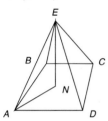

Looking down on the base $ABCD$:

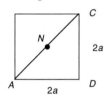

By Pythagoras $AC^2 = 4a^2 + 4a^2 = 8a^2$

$\Rightarrow AC = \sqrt{8a^2} = 2a\sqrt{2}$

Since $AN = \frac{1}{2} AC$, $AN = a\sqrt{2}$

Taking the triangle AEN:

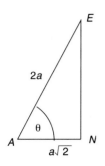

and the angle θ that we want is given by:

$$\cos \theta = \frac{a\sqrt{2}}{2a} = \frac{\sqrt{2}}{2} \Rightarrow \theta = 45°$$

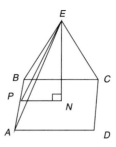

(A quicker way would have been to look at the triangle AEC, show that AEC is $90°$ by Pythagoras, then required angle is $45°$ since isosceles, but the given solution illustrates the general method.)

c The line of intersection of the planes is AB, so we take the mid-point, P say, of AB. Since Δ AEB is equilateral, PE is perpendicular to the line AB:

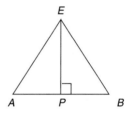

and along the base, PN is perpendicular to AB. So we take the triangle PEN to find the required angle EPN:

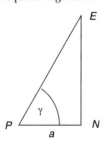

Looking at the triangle EAN in part **b,** since θ is $45°$, the triangle EAN is isosceles and so

$EN = AN = a\sqrt{2}$

This gives $\tan \gamma = \frac{a\sqrt{2}}{a} = \sqrt{2} \Rightarrow \gamma = 54.7°$ (1 d.p.)

6

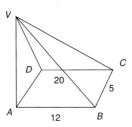

a The line of intersection of the planes is *DC* and in fact *D* is the point that we choose, since *DV* is at right angles to *DC*, as is *DA*. Taking the triangle *VAD*:

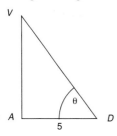

we need *VA*. Since Δ *VAB* is also right-angled, we can find *VA* from this:

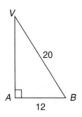

It's a 3-4-5 Δ, so *VA* is 4 × 4 = 16 cm.

This gives $\tan \theta = \frac{16}{5} \Rightarrow \theta = 72.6°$ (1 d.p.)

b Move *AB* parallel to *DC*, then look at the right-angled Δ *VCD*. We need the length of *VD*, which we can find from Δ *VAD* in the first part:

$$VD^2 = VA^2 + AD^2 = 16^2 + 5^2 = 281 \Rightarrow VD = \sqrt{281}$$

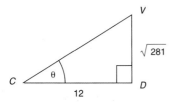

then $\tan \theta = \frac{\sqrt{281}}{12} \Rightarrow \theta = 54.4°$

7

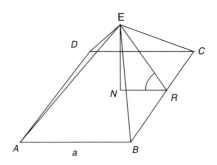

If *N* is the middle of the square base and *R* the mid-point of *BC*, we're given that *ERN* = 60°

a Since $RN = \frac{1}{2} AB = \frac{1}{2}a$

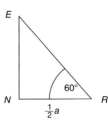

$$\tan 60° = \frac{EN}{\frac{1}{2}a}$$

$$\Rightarrow EN = \frac{1}{2}a \tan 60° = \frac{a}{2}\sqrt{3}, \text{ the height.}$$

b Looking down on the base *ABCD*:

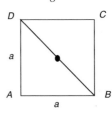

$$BD^2 = a^2 + a^2 = 2a^2 \Rightarrow BD = a\sqrt{2} \Rightarrow BN = \frac{a\sqrt{2}}{2}$$

Take triangle *ENB*:

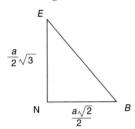

By Pythagoras,

$$EB^2 = EN^2 + BN^2 = \frac{3a^2}{4} + \frac{2a^2}{4}$$

$$= \frac{5a^2}{4} \quad \Rightarrow EB = \frac{a\sqrt5}{2}$$

c $\tan E\hat BN = \frac{a\sqrt3}{2} \div \frac{a\sqrt2}{2} = \frac{\sqrt3}{\sqrt2} \Rightarrow E\hat BN = 50.8°$

d

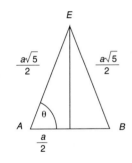

$$E\hat AB = \frac{a}{2} \div \frac{a\sqrt5}{2} = \frac{1}{\sqrt5}$$

Since $\cos^2 E\hat AB + \sin^2 E\hat AB = 1$,

$$\frac{1}{5} + \sin^2 E\hat AB = 1$$

Then $\sin^2 E\hat AB = 1 - \frac{1}{5} = \frac{4}{5}$

and $\sin E\hat AB = \frac{2}{\sqrt5}$

e   Take the triangle *EAB*:

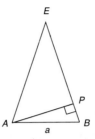

Since $\triangle EAB$ is isosceles, $E\hat AB = E\hat BA$.
Then from the right-angled $\triangle PAB$,

$$\sin P\hat BA = \frac{PA}{AB} \Rightarrow PA = AB \times \sin P\hat BA$$

$$= a \sin P\hat BA$$

But from part **d**, $\sin P\hat BA = \frac{2}{\sqrt5}$

$$PA = \frac{2a}{\sqrt5}$$

f   Since $\triangle EAB$ is congruent to $\triangle EBC$,
PC is also $\frac{2a}{\sqrt5}$

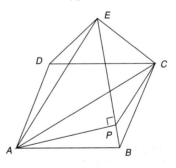

and the angle we need is $A\hat PC$. Taking the
isosceles triangle *APC*:

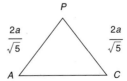

We need *AC*, which we've seen from **b** is $a\sqrt2$.
Using the cos rule:

$$\cos A\hat{P}C = \frac{PA^2 + PC^2 - AC^2}{2PA.PC} = \frac{\frac{4a^2}{5} + \frac{4a^2}{5} - 2a^2}{2 \times \frac{2a}{\sqrt{5}} \times \frac{2a}{\sqrt{5}}}$$

$$= \frac{\frac{-2a^2}{5}}{\frac{8a^2}{5}} = \frac{-1}{4}$$

8 **a** $x = 1$ **b** $x = -1$ **c** $x = 1$ and $x = -4$

   d $x = 3$ and $x = -2$

9 **a** $y \to 0$ **b** $y \to 1$ **c** $y \to 0$ **d** $y \to 0$

10 **a** The asymptotes for this curve are at $x = 1$ and $y = 0$

   when $x = 0$, $y = -1$

   $y = 0$, there are no solutions for x.

   Looking at the x-asymptote, if $x > 1$, y is +ve

   $x < 1$, y is −ve

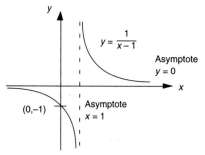

$y = \frac{1}{x-1}$

Asymptote
$y = 0$

Asymptote
$x = 1$

$(0,-1)$

   b Asymptotes at $x = -1$ and $y = 1$

   If $x = 0$, $y = 0$ and if $y = 0$, $x = 0$.

   When $x < -1$, y is $\frac{-ve}{-ve}$, +ve altogether

   $x > -1$, y is $\frac{-ve}{+ve}$, −ve altogether

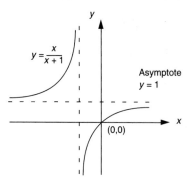

$y = \frac{x}{x+1}$

Asymptote
$y = 1$

$(0,0)$

   c Asymptotes at $x = -2$ and $y = -1$

   When $x = 0$, $y = 1$; when $y = 0$, $x = 2$

   When $x < -2$ (e.g. −2.1), y is $\frac{-ve}{-ve}$, is −ve altogether

   $x > -2$ (e.g. −1.9), y is $\frac{+ve}{+ve}$, +ve altogether

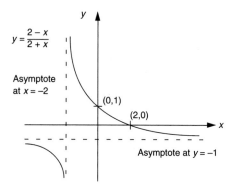

$y = \frac{2-x}{2+x}$

Asymptote
at $x = -2$

$(0,1)$

$(2,0)$

Asymptote at $y = -1$

   d Asymptotes at $x = \frac{2}{3}$ and $y = \frac{-2}{3}$

   When $x = 0$, $y = \frac{3}{2}$; when $y = 0$, $x = \frac{-3}{2}$

   When $x > \frac{2}{3}$, y is $\frac{+ve}{-ve}$, −ve

   $x < \frac{2}{3}$, y is $\frac{+ve}{+ve}$, +ve

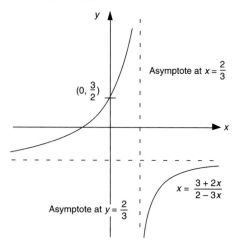

Asymptote at $x = \frac{2}{3}$

$(0, \frac{3}{2})$

$x = \frac{3 + 2x}{2 - 3x}$

Asymptote at $y = \frac{2}{3}$

11 $\frac{dy}{dx} = \frac{(1 + x^2)\,1 - x\,(2x)}{(1 + x^2)^2} = 0$ for turning points

   i.e. $1 + x^2 - 2x^2 = 0 \Rightarrow x^2 = 1 \Rightarrow x = \pm 1$

   $\frac{dy}{dx} = \frac{1 - x^2}{(1 + x^2)^2}$

when $x = 1^+$, e.g. 1.1 $\dfrac{dy}{dx} < 0$

$x = 1^-$, e.g. 0.9 $\dfrac{dy}{dx} > 0$

$/\frown\backslash$ MAX

when $x = -1^+$, e.g. -0.9 $\dfrac{dy}{dx} > 0$

$x = -1^-$, e.g. -1.1 $\dfrac{dy}{dx} < 0$

$\backslash\_/$ MIN

$x = 0 \qquad y = 0$

$y = 0 \qquad x = 0$

$\dfrac{dy}{dx} = 1$, i.e. passes through origin at $45°$

As $x \to \infty$, $y \to 0$

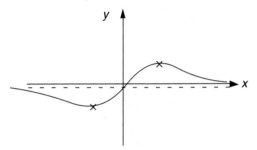

Section 10

1   **a** $\dfrac{7!}{3!4!} = 35$

2   **a** $\dfrac{4!}{3!1!}(3x)^3 = 4 \times 27x^3 = 108x^3$

    b $\dfrac{5!}{2!3!}(7x)^2 = 10 \times 49x^2 = 490x^2$

    c $\dfrac{6!}{4!2!}\left(\dfrac{x}{2}\right)^4 = 15 \times \dfrac{x^4}{16} = \dfrac{15x^4}{16}$

    d $\dfrac{5!}{5!0!}(-2x)^5 = 1 \times -32x^5 = 32x^5$

    e   Term is $\dfrac{7!}{2!5!}(-x)^2 = 21x^2$

    so coefficient is 21

    f $\dfrac{5!}{4!1!}\left(-\dfrac{x}{2}\right)^4 \ = 5 \ \times \dfrac{x^4}{16}$

    so coefficient is $\dfrac{5}{16}$

3   **a** $2^6 + 6 \times 2^5(-x) + 15 \times 2^4(-x)^2$

      $= 64 - 192x + 240x^2$

    b $(64 - 192x + 240x^2)(2 + x)$

      $= 128 - 384x + 480x^2 + 64x - 192x^2 + \ldots$

      $= 128 - 448x + 288x^2$

4 $^5C_3\,2^2(3a)^3 = 10 \times 4 \times 27a^3 = 1080a^3$

    Coefficient is 1080.

5 $1 + 6ax + 15a^2x^2$

    $(1 + bx)(1 + 6ax + 15a^2x^2)$

         $= 1 + 6ax + 15a^2x^2 + bx + 6abx^2 + \ldots$

         $= 1 + x[6a + b] + x^2[15a^2 + 6ab]$

    Equating coefficients, $6a + b = 0$ [1]

    $15a^2 + 6ab = \dfrac{-21}{4}$[2]

    From [1], $b = -6a \Rightarrow 15a^2 - 36a^2 = \dfrac{-21}{4}$

      $\Rightarrow -21a^2 = \dfrac{-21}{4}$

      $a^2 = \dfrac{1}{4} \Rightarrow \begin{matrix} a = \pm\dfrac{1}{2} \\ b = \mp\,3 \end{matrix}$

6 $1 - 10x + 40x^2$

$(a + bx)(1 - 10x + 40x^2)$
$$= a - 10ax + 40ax^2 + bx - 10bx^2 + \dots$$
$$= a + x[b - 10a] + x^2[40a - 10b]$$

Equating coefficients, $a = 2$, $b - 10a = c$
and $40a - 10b = 10$
$\Rightarrow 10b = 40a - 10 = 70$

$\Rightarrow b = 7$

$\Rightarrow c = 7 - 20 = -13$

7 Writing $f(x) = x^3 - 5x + 1$

then $f(2) = 8 - 10 + 1 = -1$

$f(3) = 27 - 15 + 1 = 13$

so there is a root between 2 and 3

with $x_0 = 2$

$x_1 = 2.080$

$x_2 = 2.110$

$x_3 = 2.122$

$x_4 = 2.126$

$x_5 = 2.128$

$x_6 = 2.128$

This is slow convergence to the root at 2.128 (3 d.p.s)

8 Putting $f(x) = x + \ln(4 + x)$

$f(-1.1) = -0.04$

$f(-1) = +0.10$

The change in sign of $f(x)$ shows a root between -1.1 and -1.

$x_0 = -1$

$x_1 = -1.099$

$x_2 = -1.065$

$x_3 = -1.077$

$x_4 = -1.073$

$x_5 = -1.074$

$x_6 = -1.074$

so the root is -1.074 (3 d.p's)

Section 11

1 We can set up a tally for the groups

200–209	||	2
210–219	||||	4
220–229	LHT LHT	10
230–239	LHT LHT ||||	14
240–249	LHT ||	7
250–259	|||	3

and check that the sum is correct! 40

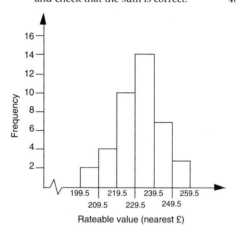

Rateable value (nearest £)

The break in the horizontal axis shows the break in values from the origin. Note that the boundaries for the histogram are half way between the limits below and above.

2 The test here is to check that the correct height is used with unequal group sizes. The sizes are respectively 10, 5, 5, 10, 20 so if we take the standard width to be 5, we need the first class to be half-height, second normal, third normal, fourth half-height, fifth quarter-height, i.e. the table becomes:

Mass	60–69	70–74	75–79	80–89	90–109
Number	3	12	25	22	18
Height	$1\frac{1}{2}$	12	25	11	$4\frac{1}{2}$

with corresponding histogram:

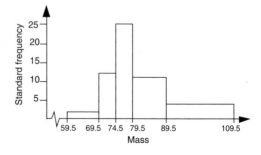

Mass

3 $\sum x_i = 220 \ n = 5 \Rightarrow \bar{x} = \dfrac{\sum x_i}{n} = \dfrac{220}{5} = 44$

$\sum x_i^2 = 10400 \Rightarrow$ variance $= \dfrac{10400}{5} - 44^2 = 144$

$\Rightarrow$ standard deviation $= \sqrt{\text{variance}} = 12$

4   **a** $\bar{x} = \dfrac{\sum x_i f_i}{\sum f_i} \Rightarrow 5 = \dfrac{2 \times 1 + 5 \times 2 + 7 \times 4 + 6 \times n}{20}$

$\Rightarrow 100 = 40 + 6n \Rightarrow x = 10$

b   Variance $= \dfrac{\sum x_i^2 f_i}{\sum f_i} - \bar{x}^2$

$= \dfrac{2 \times 1^2 + 5 \times 2^2 + 7 \times 4^2 + 6 \times 10^2}{20} - 5^2$

$= 36.7 - 25 = 11.7$

5   Tally

1	2	3	4	5	6	7	8	9
IIII	ЖҤ	ЖҤ	ЖҤ	ЖҤ	ЖҤ	ЖҤ	ЖҤ	ЖҤ
	III	ЖҤ	ЖҤ	ЖҤ	ЖҤ	ЖҤ	ЖҤ	II
		II ·	ЖҤ	ЖҤ	IIII	I		
			IIII					
4	8	12	15	19	14	11	10	7 = 100

i.e.

Age	1	2	3	4	5	6	7	8	9
Frequency	4	8	12	15	19	14	11	10	7

$\Rightarrow \bar{x} = \dfrac{4 + 16 + 36 + 60 + 95 + 84 + 77 + 80 + 63}{100}$

$= \dfrac{515}{100} = 5.15$

Variance $=$

$\dfrac{4 + 32 + 108 + 240 + 475 + 504 + 539 + 640 + 567}{100} - 5.15^2$

$= 4.57$ (2 d.p.) $\Rightarrow$ S.Dev $= 2.14$ (2 d.p.)

6   **a**   Assuming the mid-point to represent the class, the first class has boundaries $0 \to 9.5$ $\Rightarrow$ mid-point is 4.75.

The next class has boundaries 9.5 to 19.5 $\Rightarrow$ mid-point is 14.5 and so on.

The table could be set out:

Mid-point							
4.75	14.5	34.5	74.5	124.5	174.5	349.5	624.5
44	194	157	131	69	40	58	7
Frequency							

$\Rightarrow \bar{x} = \dfrac{58411}{700} = 83.44$ (2 d.p.)

Variance $= 18654 - \bar{x}^2 = 11692$

$\Rightarrow$ S. Deviation is 108.1 (1 d.p.)

b   Most of the data is grouped towards the beginning – the last invoices have a disproportionate effect. If the data is not roughly symmetrical, might be better to use the median and the interquartile range.

7   **a**   Lie between 2.45 and 2.95

Mass (kg)

<1.45	<1.95	<2.45	<2.95	<3.45	<3.95	<4.45
2	8	25	85	180	240	250

Cumulative frequency

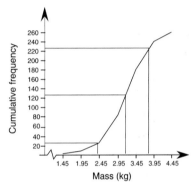

b   Median – look for value at $\sim \dfrac{250}{2}$

$= 125 \sim 3.15$ kg

c $10\% \Rightarrow$ value at $\sim \dfrac{250}{10} = 25 \Rightarrow 2.37$ kg

$90\% \Rightarrow$ value at $\sim 9 \times \dfrac{250}{10} = 225 \Rightarrow 3.80$ kg

Difference, the interpercentile range, is ~ 1.4 kg (1 d.p.)

8   The multiples of 3 are 3, 6, 9, …, 30, numbering 10

The multiples of 11 are 11, 22, numbering 2

There is no overlap

$\Rightarrow$ P(Multiple 3 or Multiple 11) $= \dfrac{10 + 2}{30} = \dfrac{2}{5}$

b   Multiples of 5 are 5, 10, …, 30, numbering 6

Multiples of 3 and 5, i.e. 15, are 15, 30, numbering 2

P(Multiple 3 $\cup$ Multiple 5)
$=$ P(Multiple 3) $+$ P(Multiple 5) $-$ P(both)

$= \dfrac{10}{30} + \dfrac{6}{30} - \dfrac{2}{30} = \dfrac{14}{30} = \dfrac{7}{15}$

9   A tree diagram would be suitable:

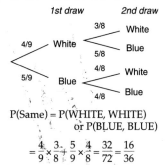

1st draw   2nd draw

P(Same) = P(WHITE, WHITE)
           or P(BLUE, BLUE)

$$= \frac{4}{9} \times \frac{3}{8} + \frac{5}{9} \times \frac{4}{8} = \frac{32}{72} = \frac{16}{36}$$

10   Another tree diagram:

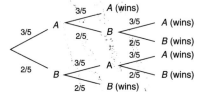

a   P(2 games finish) = P(AA) or P(BB)

$$= \frac{3}{5} \times \frac{3}{5} + \frac{2}{5} \times \frac{2}{5} = \frac{13}{25}$$

b   P(A wins) = P(AA) or P(ABA) or P(BAA)

$$= \frac{9}{25} + \frac{18}{125} + \frac{18}{125} = \frac{81}{125}$$

c   P(2 games | A wins)

$$= \frac{P(2 \text{ games} \cap A \text{ wins})}{P(A \text{ wins})} = \frac{\frac{9}{25}}{\frac{81}{125}} = \frac{5}{9}$$